Ensuring Learning

Ensuring Learning

Supporting Faculty to Improve Student Success

Christine Harrington

AMERICAN
ASSOCIATION OF
COMMUNITY
COLLEGES

ROWMAN & LITTLEFIELD
Lanham • Boulder • New York • London

Published by Rowman & Littlefield
An imprint of The Rowman & Littlefield Publishing Group, Inc.
4501 Forbes Boulevard, Suite 200, Lanham, Maryland 20706
www.rowman.com

6 Tinworth Street, London SE11 5AL, United Kingdom

British Library Cataloguing in Publication Information Available

Library of Congress Cataloging-in-Publication Data

Names: Harrington, Christine, 1971- author.
Title: Ensuring learning : supporting faculty to improve student success / Christine Harrington.
Description: Lanham : Rowman & Littlefield, [2020] | Includes bibliographical references. | Summary: "In this book, Christine Harrington shares institutional strategies that colleges can employ to increase support to faculty"—Provided by publisher.
Identifiers: LCCN 2019059362 (print) | LCCN 2019059363 (ebook) | ISBN 9781475851878 (cloth) | ISBN 9781475851885 (paperback) | ISBN 9781475851892 (epub)
Subjects: LCSH: Community college teachers—United States. | Community college teaching—United States. | Teacher effectiveness—United States. | Career development—United States. | Community colleges—Curricula—United States. | Academic achievement—United States.
Classification: LCC LB2331.72 .H37 2020 (print) | LCC LB2331.72 (ebook) | DDC 378.1/2—dc23
LC record available at https://lccn.loc.gov/2019059362
LC ebook record available at https://lccn.loc.gov/2019059363

♾ ™ The paper used in this publication meets the minimum requirements of American
National Standard for Information Sciences Permanence of Paper for Printed Library
Materials, ANSI/NISO Z39.48-1992.

Contents

Foreword

This book, the second of a series on teaching and learning by Christine Harrington, offers an evidence-based and detailed road map for faculty leaders, administrators, and those leading the education of our next generation of community colleges to build important pieces of the foundation necessary for a culture of teaching and learning excellence to flourish. It also offers a much-needed framework to articulate an underdeveloped part of the guided pathways approach—the fourth pillar on "ensuring students are learning" that is sweeping across the country to help our colleges organize their student success redesign efforts.

Faculty have always been and will always be the first and most important contact with our students. I included that statement in a lecture I delivered in 2018 at North Carolina State University's College of Education, making an urgent case for "Focusing the Next Generation of Community College Redesign on Teaching and Learning." In that lecture I called for leaders to empower faculty to lead changes in pedagogy, to rethink and align course and program outcomes, and to build coherent and clear course and program sequences. I also articulated a case for investing in and designing campus-based Centers for Teaching and Learning to serve as a hub for supporting and catalyzing faculty leadership in the building of a culture of teaching and learning excellence; a culture that must center our efforts to redesign our community colleges to improve student outcomes at scale.

This book underscores the need for faculty to lead this culture building around teaching and learning excellence. Each of the chapters covers foundational elements such as program and course learning outcomes, a case for backward course design, evidenced-based teaching and learning practices, and assessing instructor effectiveness. These drive the redesign of our nation's community colleges around teaching and learning. The first chapter offers a road map for starting a Center for Teaching and Learning, including offering suggestions for how a Center should craft a mission, staff the work, build programming, engage part-time faculty, and adopt mentoring programs to support faculty growth. The idea of the Teaching and Learning Center, and how it can support the development of a culture of teaching and learning excellence, is also threaded into every chapter.

The author also offers a number of essential points on often overlooked pieces of our teaching and learning culture. For example, the chapter on program and course learning outcomes and assessment speaks to the importance of helping faculty understand how assessment really does support their work with students. It also speaks to the essential role institutional research plays in supporting assessment and points to our lack of training in assessment as a barrier to connecting it fully to the improvement of teaching and to resulting changes in student achievement.

This is a must-read for community colleges committed to building the foundation necessary to create a culture of teaching and learning on their campuses.

Dr. Karen A. Stout
President and CEO, Achieving the Dream
President Emerita, Montgomery County Community College, PA

Preface

Completion rates at many colleges and universities across the nation, especially at community colleges, are unacceptably low. Significant equity gaps exist for students of color and students from low-income backgrounds. Fortunately, colleges are engaging in important and courageous conversations about institutional changes that are needed to improve student success outcomes.

Guided pathways is a national movement focused on improving student success that has gained significant traction and is serving as a framework for institutional change. Guided pathways thought leaders have identified four essential practices: determining paths, helping students choose a path, helping students stay on the path, and ensuring learning. The first three essential practices have been the focus of national conversations and conferences.

Ensuring learning, the fourth essential practice, has unfortunately not received as much attention. When I served a two-year term as the executive director for the Center for Student Success at the New Jersey Council of County Colleges, I had numerous opportunities to engage in national-level conversations and attended countless conferences and policy meetings about guided pathways. Ensuring learning was usually only briefly mentioned, if at all, in these conversations and conferences.

The only guaranteed shared experience for college students is the classroom experience. Students spend hundreds of hours each year participating in face-to-face and virtual classes. Faculty are the ones who students interact with the most, both in and out of the classroom. In order to improve student success outcomes, significant attention to the classroom experience is needed.

One of the best ways for institutions to improve student success outcomes is by supporting faculty. Faculty are typically hired for their content expertise and may have little, if any, formal training in how to effectively teach. Many seasoned faculty have developed expertise through trial-and-error processes, but this approach to high-quality teaching takes time. Hundreds of thousands of students are taking classes with faculty with limited experiences and expertise. Supporting early-career faculty and part-time faculty is particularly important. However, all faculty can benefit from support and professional development opportunities.

Providing significant support and resources to full and part-time faculty will undoubtedly lead to improved learning and achievement. Faculty are eager to improve their teaching. When I served as the director of the Center for the Enrichment of Learning and Teaching at Middlesex County College and as the executive director of the Center for Student Success at the New Jersey Council of County Colleges, full and part-time faculty were appreciative of the professional development opportunities offered. Hundreds of faculty took advantage of these programs and many reported back with examples of how they transformed their teaching practices as a result of participating.

Unfortunately, many colleges only offer limited support to faculty. I was shocked to discover how many community colleges do not even have a Teaching and Learning Center. Many faculty report having little-to-no funding to attend conferences and other professional development opportunities.

Community colleges tout themselves as being teaching-focused. However, supports for developing effective teachers are not always in place. Professional development for faculty is often quite limited in scope and duration, and part-time faculty may not even be invited to participate.

I wrote this book to bring attention to the fourth and perhaps most important essential practice of guided pathways—ensuring learning. Teaching and learning need to take center stage in our conversations on student success reform. By increasing support for faculty and improving teaching and learning practices, students will learn and achieve more. I am hopeful that college leaders will find the institutional strategies and approaches to supporting full and part-time faculty helpful as they strive to ensure that students are learning and achieving on their campuses.

Ensuring Learning: Supporting Faculty to Improve Student Success is the second book in a two-book series focused on engaging and supporting faculty. In the first book, *Engaging Faculty in Guided Pathways: A Practical Resource for College Leaders,* I highlight the faculty role in all four essential practices of guided pathways and strategies to increase faculty participation and engagement. I am hopeful that college leaders will find the summaries of the tasks, engagement strategies, and reflection questions for each essential practice of guided pathways to be helpful as they determine the best way to engage and empower full and part-time faculty at their institution.

The first book in this series, *Engaging Faculty in Guided Pathways* is comprised of the following chapters:

Chapter 1: Determining Paths
Chapter 2: Helping Students Choose a Path
Chapter 3: Helping Students Stay on the Path
Chapter 4: Ensuring Learning
Chapter 5: Faculty at the Table: Departmental and Institutional-Level Conversations
Chapter 6: Leadership Development

After reading *Engaging Faculty in Guided Pathways*, you will be able to:

1. Describe the role of faculty in determining paths.
2. Determine strategies to engage faculty in determining career clusters and developing program maps.
3. Describe the role of faculty in helping students choose a path.
4. Determine strategies to engage faculty in incorporating career exploration into curriculum and advising.
5. Describe the role of faculty in helping students stay on the path.
6. Determine strategies to engage faculty in helping students overcome academic and non-academic challenges.
7. Describe the role of faculty in ensuring learning.
8. Determine strategies to engage faculty in assessment, course design, and evidence-based practices.
9. Discuss strategies to engage faculty in guided pathways through departmental conversations.
10. Identify strategies to gain faculty voice in institutional conversations on student success.
11. Describe approaches and models for faculty engagement in formal leadership training and development.
12. Determine how to use mentoring to facilitate leadership skill development among faculty.

Ensuring Learning: Supporting Faculty to Improve Student Success is a deep dive into the fourth essential practice of guided pathways—ensuring learning. In this book, I share institutional strategies that colleges can employ to increase support to faculty. More specifically, I describe the importance of Teaching and Learning Centers and provide guidance on how institutions can start or enhance Centers focused on improving teaching and learning. I also provide strategies to increase faculty engagement with program and course-level assessment and discuss how professional development can assist faculty with effective course design and implementation. Finally, the importance of using assessment of instructor effectiveness as an opportunity to improve teaching and learning is addressed.

After reading this book, you will be able to:

1. Explain why colleges should invest in a Teaching and Learning Center.
2. Describe processes related to starting a new Teaching and Learning Center.
3. Discuss various types of programs and services that can be offered by a Teaching and Learning Center.
4. Describe strategies that can be used to engage faculty in assessment.
5. Determine institutional strategies that communicate the importance of assessment.
6. Identify a professional development plan to support faculty with assessment.
7. Describe backward design and how course design impacts student learning.
8. Determine strategies to train and support faculty in backward design.
9. Explain the importance of faculty using evidence-based teaching and learning practices.
10. Discuss how colleges can support faculty with developing effective syllabi, engaging students, improving lecturing and group work, and teaching online.
11. Describe how using an improvement lens for assessing instructor effectiveness can improve student outcomes.
12. Evaluate current practices related to assessing instructor effectiveness.
13. Develop or revise processes and practices related to assessing instructor effectiveness to focus on improving teaching and learning.

Acknowledgments

Becoming a professor was never my plan. I certainly did not expect to become a national expert on teaching and learning. So how did this happen? I began working in the community college sector as a counselor and was immediately encouraged by my good friend Elaine Daidone to teach psychology courses as an adjunct. With her encouragement, I approached the psychology department and was assigned to teach Introductory Psychology. I was excited about this new opportunity, as I'm always up for a new challenge, but was also quite nervous because I only had one experience in the classroom as part of my doctoral program.

I was very fortunate that my institution started a Center for the Enrichment of Learning and Teaching soon after I started teaching. I immediately found mentors and colleagues who were willing to help me learn how to be an effective teacher. I am incredibly grateful to all my faculty colleagues. I have learned so much from so many full and part-time faculty at Middlesex County College as well as from faculty teaching at many other colleges and universities. My faculty colleagues care deeply about their students and continually strive to be better teachers. I love hearing about their innovative approaches to helping students learn.

In 2011, I was elected by my faculty peers to serve as the director for the Center for the Enrichment of Learning and Teaching. I am so grateful to Dr. Kathy Fedorko who encouraged me to run for this position. This experience transformed my teaching and played a critical role in my career. Others were relying on me to help them develop effective teaching skills. I had to quickly become an expert. After consuming the literature, attending conferences, and learning from others, I started to give back to the field by writing books on teaching and learning and presenting at local and national conferences.

The guided pathways thought leaders have sparked important national and local conversations about student success. When I took on the role of the executive director for the Center for Student Success at the New Jersey Council of County Colleges, I had the privilege of having a seat at tables where national experts strategized about how to better serve students. Most of the leaders were administrators and researchers; I was one of the few who represented the faculty voice. I am honored to be able to utilize my expertise to guide and inform these conversations. The impact we can have by improving teaching approaches is significant and far-reaching.

I would also like to take this opportunity to thank several of my colleagues who have supported me with this project. Dr. Theresa Orosz, assistant dean of the division of arts and sciences at Middlesex County College; Donna Rogalski, director of advisement and retention at Camden County College; and Dr. Michael Sparrow, dean of enrollment management and retention at Northampton Community College, all provided incredibly valuable feedback that helped shape the final product. I am grateful for their time, expertise, and friendship.

You can't go on this journey without a strong support system. Writing a book is an overwhelming and time-consuming task. I am very fortunate to have an incredibly supportive family. Thank you to my husband, Dan, and my two sons, Ryan and David, for always being there to encourage and support me.

Introduction

In response to then-President Obama's education agenda and challenge for community colleges to educate an additional five million students with degrees, certificates, or other credentials by 2020, the American Association of Community Colleges (AACC) embarked on its 21st Century Initiative to lead the nation's efforts in increasing the focus on student success and completion. Community colleges were well known for their ability to provide access to quality higher education that was affordable and flexible but this call to action spoke to the need for students to complete and succeed in order to ensure the nation's middle class continued to thrive in the twenty-first century and beyond.

The 21st Century Initiative brought together the best and brightest from across the community college sector to listen and gather information from stakeholders and determine ways to tackle challenges impeding student success. It was ambitious to say the least. Members of the team developed recommendations that included:

- increasing focus and building momentum for the community college completion agenda and identifying AACC's role in that effort;
- promoting the contributions and challenges of community colleges among the public, policymakers, and business leaders; and
- building support for accuracy and accountability in monitoring community college performance.

More than recommendations, the 21st Century Initiative created and tasked implementation teams to develop specific strategies and model action plans that would serve as a guide to colleges. One of those recommendations was the AACC Pathways Initiative. AACC Pathways Initiative was a major project focused on helping community colleges design and implement structured academic and career pathways to completion for all students. AACC's president and CEO Walter G. Bumphus noted that AACC's Pathways was a game changer not only for implementing clear outlines for students to follow but for AACC to develop and produce models, training, and materials based upon successful programs to serve as guidelines for local implementation. In other words, AACC Pathways was set up to create replicable and scalable ways for colleges across the nation to increase student success.

Community colleges that have begun to implement Pathways know that it is no small undertaking and requires a committed, diverse, and willing local team. At the heart of the student experience are the faculty and they are just as crucial to the success of any institutional change but especially in implementing Pathways. In fact, community college presidents have noted that faculty are essential in leading, implementing, and evaluating the structures and processes needed for Pathways. It is the faculty experience and expertise that help to ensure that Pathways is sustainable and not simply another initiative.

Since the 21st Century Initiative, AACC and a group of committed and experienced partners were able to launch national efforts that have shifted the collective focus and national discussions about student success and completion. A pathway itself, the AACC Pathways Initiative is an outline for sustainable institutional transformation that, at its core, seeks to positively impact the twelve million students served by the American community college system and set them up for success.

Martha M. Parham, EdD
Sr. Vice President, Public Relations
American Association of Community Colleges

Chapter One

Teaching and Learning Centers

At the end of this chapter, you will be able to:

1. Explain why colleges should invest in a Teaching and Learning Center.
2. Describe processes related to starting a new Teaching and Learning Center.
3. Discuss various types of programs and services that can be offered by a Teaching and Learning Center.

Faculty do not typically have training in how to be an effective teacher. Graduate programs designed to prepare faculty for the world of academia typically focus on preparing students to be scholars in their discipline. Most graduate programs are specifically focused on preparing students to secure faculty positions at four-year institutions (Rhoades, 2012). Because research is the primary responsibility for faculty at many of these institutions, it is not surprising that teaching has not been an area of focus in graduate programs.

Fortunately, some graduate programs are starting to turn more attention to teaching practices and offer, or even require, courses on how to teach effectively. However, even in programs where courses on pedagogy and andragogy are taught, it is still a relatively small part of the overall curriculum. Furthermore, it is likely that faculty who graduated many years ago have not taken a single course on how to teach. Thus, faculty are expected to teach despite not having any formal training in how to do so effectively.

The student experience in the classroom really matters. Students who experience success, gain confidence, believe in their ability to succeed, and have a sense of belonging in the classroom are most likely to continue in college and perform well (Center for Community College Student Engagement, 2019; Komarraju & Nadler, 2013). On the other hand, students who experience failure are likely to have lower levels of self-efficacy and are more likely to drop out of college. Faculty can play a critical role in fostering self-efficacy and student success.

In order to positively impact teaching and learning practices and tackle the ensuring learning essential practice of guided pathways, colleges need to provide high-quality, ongoing professional development to faculty. Brown and Kurzweil (2018) note there is "robust literature on the relationship between constructs of instructor quality and student outcomes such as course success, retention, and degree completion" (p. 8). Van den Bergh, Ros, and Beijaard (2014), for instance, found that instructors who attended professional development put what they learned into practice. The results of this study indicate that professional development leads to changes in both teacher attitudes and behaviors.

In a study conducted by Perez, McShannon, and Hynes (2012), it was found that student success outcomes improved when faculty teaching at a community college participated in a semester-long professional development program; specifically, retention improved by 4% and overall success by almost 8%. What makes these outcomes even more impressive is that 70% of the student population identified as a minority.

Many colleges have developed Teaching and Learning Centers to spearhead faculty development efforts. Beach, Sorcinelli, Austin, and Rivard (2016) report that the number of formal, centralized Teaching and Learning Centers across the nation continues to climb, especially at community colleges. Directors and staff of Teaching and Learning Centers are being called upon to act as change agents to transform teaching and learning practices, an essential practice in the guided pathways movement.

One important way that Teaching and Learning Center directors can function as change agents is what Schroeder (2011) refers to as "getting at the table." She emphasizes that Teaching and Learning Center directors must provide both instructional and institutional support. Thus, in addition to developing and implementing professional development programs, Teaching and Learning Center directors should utilize their teaching and learning expertise to be involved in institutional decision-making. During institutional meetings, Teaching and Learning Center directors can ensure that teaching and learning remain at the forefront of institutional priorities.

INVESTING IN A TEACHING AND LEARNING CENTER

Senior-level administrative support for Teaching and Learning Centers is critical (Forgie, Yonge, & Luth, 2018). Gurung, Ansburg, Alexander, Lawrence, and Johnson (2008) note that a lack of high-level support from administrators was identified as a major obstacle to changing campus culture and faculty behaviors related to teaching and learning. The necessity of Teaching and Learning Centers and professional development for faculty needs to be explicitly communicated by top-level administrators at meetings and other media outlets such as websites and newsletters. Clearly identifying teaching and learning as a priority in the strategic plan is needed for transformational change to occur.

At a recent conference, Pando (2019) stated that one of the best ways senior administrators can communicate institutional priorities is through the budget. Wyner (2019) notes that "if the president doesn't convey the importance of exceptional teaching and learning and align the institution's resources toward that goal, nobody will, and the exceptional teaching practices of great faculty will never scale" (para. 6). It is therefore important for college leaders to keep teaching and learning at the forefront of budget decisions.

Colleges with limited and declining budgets are faced with many difficult decisions. Budget cuts have unfortunately become the norm at many colleges, especially community colleges. It is unfortunate that budget challenges often result in eliminating or significantly reducing budget line items related to hiring new faculty and providing professional development.

According to Brown and Kurzweil (2018), investing in teaching and learning by hiring talented faculty and supporting current faculty often results in increased revenue because "instructional quality is positively associated with student retention" (p. 5). They note that the cost of retaining a student is significantly lower than the cost of recruiting a new student. The same applies to the recruitment and retention of faculty, especially faculty from underrepresented populations.

In their call for action, the League for Innovation in the Community College (2018) strongly advises colleges to find creative ways to allocate funds and time for both full and part-time faculty to become better teachers. Teaching and Learning Centers can be the hub for faculty to work collaboratively to improve teaching practices. Although investing in a Teaching and Learning Center will certainly have up-front costs, the return on investment is high. Through improved teaching and learning practices, student success outcomes will undoubtedly improve.

According to a national survey of Teaching and Learning Center directors, most Centers are operating on budgets of less than $100,000, excluding salaries (Beach et al., 2016). Not surprisingly, results from this study show that Teaching and Learning Centers at community colleges tend to have the lowest budgets. More than one-third of the centers at community colleges operate with budgets less than $25,000 and 59% have budgets under $50,000 (Beach et al., 2016).

In-house professional development is more cost-effective than sending faculty to conferences; however, a combination of internal and external professional development will likely lead to the best outcomes. Teaching and Learning Centers can offer the platform for full and part-time faculty to share their expertise with colleagues. In addition to using internal talent, inviting the entire faculty body to presentations or workshops given by national experts is also an effective way to stretch professional development dollars.

Colleges will want to determine what financial reward structures need to be in place to ensure faculty participation is high at professional development events. Stout (2018) emphasizes the need to consider reward structures for part-time faculty participation. Compensating faculty for their time is one approach but this may be cost prohibitive at some colleges.

Kisker (2019) cautions colleges to consider the sustainability of providing funds to faculty for attending professional development. Although compensating faculty for their time can serve as an incentive, college leaders need to determine if this is a financially viable approach for the long term. Other approaches can include rewarding professional development through raises associated with different rank levels or priority and consistent scheduling (Fuller, 2017).

Despite their value, colleges will not want to rely exclusively on internal approaches to professional development. There are significant benefits to sending faculty to local, regional, and national conferences, especially when there is a special emphasis on teaching and learning. These conferences give faculty an opportunity to witness how other colleges are implementing evidence-based practices and connect with colleagues who teach in the same or similar disciplines.

Faculty who attend these external professional development opportunities come back refreshed and with many new ideas about how to improve student learning. In addition, professional networking enables faculty to expand on their current support team. Funds for external professional development have traditionally been limited and sometimes nonexistent. This is especially true for part-time faculty. Colleges will need to find creative ways, including exploring grants, to fund these important professional development activities in order to improve student success rates.

Staffing the Teaching and Learning Center is expensive but a critical investment. Having a talented leadership team is a must. Release time is a relatively inexpensive investment and provides team members with the time needed to develop expertise to design and implement professional development programming. Many Teaching and Learning Centers have faculty fellows who serve on the team and receive release time to lead various efforts such as new faculty mentoring or faculty learning communities. Colleges using a release-time approach will likely need to recruit more talented part-time faculty to ensure coverage of classes.

After colleges determine who will be a part of the Teaching and Learning Center team, they will want to support their professional development. It cannot be assumed that talented faculty have expertise in helping others improve teaching and learning or know how to effectively lead a Center. To ensure the faculty leadership team of the Center is effective, colleges will need to provide ongoing support.

Sending the Teaching and Learning Center director and team members to local and national conferences on professional development will enable them to develop this expertise and establish the network they need to successfully run a Teaching and Learning Center. The Professional Organizational Development (POD) network is the most well-known organization in this arena. This network sponsors two conferences each year, one specifically for new faculty developers and the other for the wider membership.

Learning from others doing this work is a significant part of professional growth and development. As staff or team members of the Teaching and Learning Center become more knowledgeable about the scholarship of teaching and learning, capacity and expertise across the institution increases. Having more experts in teaching and learning will undoubtedly lead to conversations and actions aimed at improving student learning campus-wide.

Interestingly, colleges have been investing in e-learning and instructional design in significant ways. Support for online learning is also incredibly important but not more important than assisting faculty with teaching effectively in traditional face-to-face learning environments, especially since most courses offered at community colleges are taught in person. In a recent survey, 67% of students indicated they are not taking any online courses (Lederman, 2018b). As a result, colleges may want to have Teaching and Learning Centers and Instructional Design offices work collaboratively.

Many effective design and delivery methods can be used in both online and face-to-face environments. For example, backward course design is relevant and needed in all learning environments. Similarly, knowing how to provide meaningful and effective feedback is a skill that instructors need whether they teach in person or online.

Encouraging collaboration and merging offices are great ways to leverage current resources and provide one centralized place for faculty to go for instructional support (Lieberman, 2018). Haras, Taylor, Sorcinelli, and von Hoene (2017) even suggest having Information Technology Services housed in or near the Teaching and Learning Center. By investing in faculty, colleges can create a campus culture where teaching and learning are highly valued and emphasized.

ESTABLISHING A NEW TEACHING AND LEARNING CENTER

Recognizing the value of Teaching and Learning Centers, many colleges, especially those committed to the guided pathways movement, have decided to make significant investments in establishing a Teaching and Learning Center. Starting a Teaching and Learning Center can seem like a daunting task, especially if resources are scarce. However, with strong leadership, changing the campus culture to more significantly emphasize teaching and learning can be accomplished even with limited resources.

Leadership Team

The first step in launching a Teaching and Learning Center is to determine the leadership structure. Colleges will need to decide if the director of the Center will be full or part-time and whether this person will be a member of the faculty on release or in an administrative position. Recruiting a talented leader who will be respected by colleagues and is able to champion teaching and learning professional development is incredibly important. Beach et al. (2016) found that most Teaching and Learning Center directors previously held a faculty position. This academic background will be important to the faculty.

Some colleges hire or appoint a faculty member or administrator based on their prior commitment to teaching and learning and demonstrated leadership skills. Another frequently used approach is to elect a director. Elections are most commonly used at institutions where the director is a faculty release position. When the election process is used, director candidates typically write a statement explaining their interest in the position and describe their vision for the Center. Faculty members can then vote to elect the director.

Staffing models for the Teaching and Learning Center can vary from college to college. Beach et al. (2016) reported that most Teaching and Learning Centers had one director, one or two associate directors, several professional staff and support staff but noted that community college Teaching and Learning Centers typically have a director that is less than full time and perhaps one support staff.

Release time for the director position is typically half time, meaning the faculty member will still have to teach 2–3 classes each semester if teaching a 5–5 load, which is typical at community colleges. Sometimes faculty fellows are also a part of the Teaching and Learning Center staff. Faculty fellows are often receiving release time in exchange for leading efforts such as faculty learning communities. The more staff, the more robust the programming of the Center.

It is problematic that community colleges, where teaching is the primary focus, do not have as many resources devoted to improving teaching and learning. Brown and Kurzweil (2018) report that investments in teaching and learning have a high return on investment. Specifically, they note that "instructional improvement can improve student outcomes, which can, in turn, increase revenue or decrease expenditures by an amount that exceeds the cost of instructional improvement" (p. 5).

The Teaching and Learning Center director role could be a permanent position or could be a rotating position. Administrative directors are more likely to be permanent positions while faculty directors are more likely to be rotating positions with terms of approximately two to three years. There are advantages and disadvantages to each approach.

Having a permanent position provides continuity and consistency while a term-based director periodically allows for new and different perspectives and leadership styles. Too short a term, however, is not advisable as there is a steep learning curve in this position. Most colleges that use a term-approach allow faculty to be considered for a second or even third term.

As colleges grapple with the leadership approach they will use, it will also be important to draft job descriptions for the Teaching and Learning Center director and staff. Colleges will want to clearly articulate qualifications needed and job duties. Expertise in teaching and learning and the desire to learn about the scholarship of teaching and learning are often the most important characteristics of directors. Although the focus of the Teaching and Learning Center is on teaching and learning, many of the leader tasks are administrative in nature. It is therefore important that the director has strong teaching, leadership, and administrative skills.

Having a staff versus just one director is advantageous for many reasons. First, more staff means the Center can provide substantial support to all faculty. In addition, it can be very helpful for the director to have colleagues who are knowledgeable about professional development to partner with when strategizing and planning. Team members with different perspectives can add value to conversations about how to best support full and part-time faculty.

To provide additional suggestions and guidance, Teaching and Learning Centers may also want to consider establishing an advisory board. Advisory boards can be utilized to help define the vision and mission of the Teaching and Learning Center and determine the best way to achieve identified goals. In many cases, advisory board members are faculty and administrators from different departments and divisions within the institution. Part-time faculty should also be represented on the advisory board. Having representation from various constituencies can help ensure the work of the Center is meeting the needs of all faculty.

Advisory boards are typically comprised of volunteer members. Although their contributions can be quite significant, the time commitment is usually not overly burdensome. Schroeder (2011) emphasized the value of advisory board members, noting that they can be advocates for resources and programs aimed at improving teaching and learning.

Leaders will need time and space to develop confidence and expertise as this is likely a new role. Providing the director, members of the leadership team, and advisory board members with resources and time to read, discuss, and become more knowledgeable about the scholarship of teaching and learning is critical. Leaders need to be confident in order to be most effective.

Colleges may want to give the leadership team a full semester or even a year to engage in significant learning about the scholarship of teaching and learning literature and how to effectively run a Teaching and Learning Center before developing programs for the rest of the campus. Planning time is important. When colleges rush into action, this may not lead to programming that will lead to improved teaching and learning.

Vision and Mission

Once a leadership team has been established, the next order of business is to develop a vision and mission statement. There are three primary steps involved in this process: formulating, communicating, and enacting (Schroeder, 2011). To formulate the vision and mission, the leadership team, often in collaboration with the advisory board, can discuss the purpose and goal of the Teaching and Learning Center.

As Teaching and Learning Centers work on developing their vision and mission, it is important to consider the role of the Center in the context of the institutional vision, mission, and strategic plan. Teaching and Learning Center teams can ask themselves the following questions during this process:

- Why is the Teaching and Learning Center being created?
- How can the Teaching and Learning Center support institutional priorities?
- Through programs and services, what would an effective Teaching and Learning Center accomplish?
- How can the Center positively impact student success?
- What types of support do faculty need in order to increase student learning and performance?

After the vision and mission have been clearly articulated, the next step is to communicate the vision and mission to the entire campus so everyone understands the role, purpose, and scope of the Center. Zakrajsek (2016) suggests posting the Center's vision and mission statements around campus and distributing them widely. With new Teaching and Learning Centers, it is important to clearly communicate why the Center is being established and the goals of doing so.

Enacting on the vision and mission is the next step. The vision and mission should guide all the practices and activities of the Teaching and Learning Center. Every program and service offered needs to support the vision and mission. In addition to shedding light on what a Teaching and Learning Center should be doing, a clear vision and mission can also help Centers determine what not to do.

Mission creep is when Teaching and Learning Center directors or teams are asked to do activities that are not within the bounds of the mission. For example, a Teaching and Learning Center could be asked to support faculty with tenure and promotion processes. This type of support may align nicely to the vision and mission of some Teaching and Learning Centers but not others.

Having a clear vision and mission provides good direction for Teaching and Learning Center directors to determine what activities do or do not align with their stated purpose and goals. For example, most Teaching and Learning Centers do not conduct evaluative classroom observations but will conduct peer observations that focus on improving versus evaluating teaching. Focus is important when determining how to best use limited resources.

As Teaching and Learning Centers work on enacting the vision and mission, prioritization is needed. Many strategies for enactment will undoubtedly be identified, but Centers will need to consider institutional priorities and resources allocated to determine what programs and services to focus on first. Centers, especially those just getting started, may want to focus on one or two big initiatives each year, depending on resources allocated. It is important that the leadership team doesn't take on too much too quickly.

Workshops are excellent tools to help increase the visibility of the Center and its goals and can be a great way to begin. However, leadership teams will also want to offer more in-depth learning opportunities such as faculty learning communities that are most likely to lead to changes in how faculty teach. Programs need to be high-quality so that faculty find them valuable and will continue to participate. When faculty do not perceive faculty development to be useful, they opt out of participating (Behar-Horenstein, Garvin, Catalanotto, & Hudson-Vassell, 2014).

The key is to identify meaningful activities that directly align with the mission and vision of the Center and are responsive to faculty needs, but not to do too much all at once. Even if the college invests in more staff for the leadership team, it is important to remember there is a learning curve for the leaders. They will likely need to build their skills and confidence in this new leadership role before rolling out significant programs.

Giving these leaders the time and space for planning and expertise development is important. This will result in better programming. Moving the needle on student success outcomes is much more likely when faculty are supported through high-quality professional development.

TEACHING AND LEARNING CENTER PROGRAMS

Teaching and Learning Centers can provide many different types of support to faculty. Programming efforts will need to be developed with capacity and mission in mind. Teaching and Learning Centers will want to consider how the Center can support the institution's mission and strategic plan. For example, institutional goals and priorities that relate to guided pathways can be reviewed to determine how the Center can support these efforts. Developing a mission and strategic plan for the Teaching and Learning Center is also advisable as these will guide the actions of the Center.

Assessing Faculty Needs

Professional development programming will be most effective when it aligns with faculty needs. Teaching and Learning Center directors will, therefore, want to conduct a needs assessment. Surveying faculty can provide insights into what faculty are looking for help and support on. Informal feedback gathered via conversations with faculty is another way to determine priority areas for programming. Teaching and Learning Center directors can also survey those who do classroom observations to determine what professional development topics might be needed the most.

Faculty will not likely attend programs unless they believe the session will be of value to them. Unfortunately, many faculty members report attending events that were not valuable. For instance, in a study conducted by Behar-Horenstein et al. (2014), 38.4% of faculty responding to the survey indicated that the quality of previous professional development was poor or fair. When faculty have this experience, they may be less likely to attend events in the future. It is therefore important for Teaching and Learning Center directors to develop high-quality programs that address faculty concerns and are perceived as valuable.

Professional Development Workshops

The most frequently provided service by Teaching and Learning Centers is the workshop (Beach et al., 2016). This is probably because it is much easier and less time-consuming to organize and plan workshops as compared to ongoing and more in-depth professional development. Workshops or day-long events can be offered prior to the start of the semester, during the semester, or at the end of the semester.

One- or two-day professional development events at the start of the academic year are great ways to engage and motivate faculty. At these events, faculty can be introduced to new perspectives, ideas, or research. Faculty can also begin conversations that will hopefully continue throughout the academic year.

Another advantage of offering professional development at the start of the year is that the program won't conflict with teaching responsibilities because classes have not yet begun. At some colleges, faculty may even be required to attend. Professional development days at the start of the semester can inspire and motivate faculty to perhaps try a new teaching approach or modify policies and practices.

The Teaching and Learning Center can also plan in-person and online professional development workshops throughout the year. These one-hour workshops are often about teaching techniques and can take place via face-to-face or online formats such as podcasts or videos. Some Teaching and Learning Centers use a theme to connect workshop topics throughout a semester or academic year while others offer more varied programming.

Professional development days at the end of the term are often best used for reflective practices. At the end of the term, faculty can converse with colleagues about what worked well and the challenges encountered. Teaching and Learning Center staff can validate faculty challenges, offer suggestions for next semester, and encourage faculty to use the semester break to redesign courses. Perhaps the most significant benefit of faculty participating in workshops at this time of year is that they then have the summer to put what they learned into practice.

It is important that Teaching and Learning Centers do not rely exclusively on workshops. Zakrajsek (2016) notes that "there is fairly consistent evidence that one-shot workshops rarely lead to productive changes in faculty members' teaching effectiveness" (p. 101). It would obviously be difficult to transform teaching and learning via a one-hour workshop.

Significant learning requires more time on task. It should be noted though that workshops are very useful for faculty who do not want to commit to more time-consuming professional development but are interested in learning about the scholarship of teaching and learning. Workshops can also motivate faculty and generate enthusiasm for more in-depth learning opportunities that Teaching and Learning Centers provide.

Faculty Learning Communities

Cox (2004) describes faculty learning communities as small groups of faculty regularly coming together throughout the academic year to focus on a teaching and learning topic. Although the most common duration for learning communities is the entire academic year, some may only meet one semester while others may meet for more than one year. In terms of size, Cox (2004) recommends that faculty learning communities consist of approximately 8–12 faculty members, all interested in exploring a specific topic related to teaching and learning.

Teaching and Learning Centers can invite faculty to participate in a learning community and the participants can determine the topic area they would like to discuss. Another approach is for Teaching and Learning Center directors to identify a topic area based on the needs assessment that was conducted. Faculty can then elect to participate if they are interested in that specific topic.

Teaching and Learning Centers will want to provide faculty participating in learning communities with relevant resources. For example, books and journal articles related to the topic can be shared and used as a springboard for conversations. Faculty can also be encouraged to conduct research to find additional resources and share these with their colleagues.

Action should be the focus of the faculty learning community. After gaining foundational information on the teaching strategy or approach, members of the faculty learning community should be putting this knowledge into action in their classes. During meetings, faculty can discuss successes and problem-solve challenges that arise.

At the end of the learning community, faculty can showcase their new teaching skills. For example, if a faculty learning community was focused on course design, a revised syllabus could be shared and new teaching approaches could be discussed. Faculty can be encouraged to collect assessment data to determine if teaching changes resulted in increased student learning.

Because faculty learning communities are time-intensive and can only serve a small number of faculty at a time, part-time faculty are unfortunately often excluded from participating. This is problematic since more than half of the courses at community colleges are taught by part-time faculty, and research has shown that student success rates are lower for students taking courses with part-time versus full-time faculty (Ran & Bickerstaff, 2019). Colleges will want to consider ways they can invite part-time faculty to participate in these powerful professional development opportunities (Fuller, 2017).

One possible approach could be to set up virtual faculty learning communities so that it is easier for part-time faculty to participate. Part-time faculty may be teaching at several different institutions or have another full-time position and this makes attending in-person meetings difficult or impossible (Smith, 2007). When developing online faculty learning communities, Teaching and Learning Center directors should not try to replicate face-to-face learning communities but should instead design online faculty learning communities with the virtual environment in mind (Lenning, Hill, Saunders, Solan, & Stokes, 2013).

An alternative to the topic-based approach is the cohort-based approach to faculty learning communities. New faculty learning communities are probably the most common example of the cohort approach in practice. According to a national survey of Teaching and Learning Center directors, new faculty development has received increased attention and is one of the top services provided by Centers (Beach et al., 2016).

A new faculty learning community provides faculty with the opportunity to connect with other colleagues who are also transitioning into this new role. It is a great way to foster strong connections among faculty across different disciplines. Assisting faculty with developing and enhancing their teaching skills at the start of their careers will have the greatest impact on the success of their students.

Faculty learning communities have been shown to positively impact teaching and learning practices. For instance, Cox (2004) found that student learning increased as a result of faculty participation in faculty learning communities. Despite their effectiveness, Teaching and Learning Centers are still relying primarily on workshops and are only using faculty learning communities to a moderate extent (Beach et al., 2016).

Faculty want in-depth support related to teaching more effectively but say that time constraints given their heavy teaching loads and other responsibilities make it difficult to participate (Smith, 2007; League for Innovation in the Community College, 2018). To scale the positive effects of faculty learning communities, colleges will need to find ways to give faculty the time to develop teaching expertise and provide incentives so that these professional development opportunities are viewed as a priority (Gurung et al., 2008).

Colleges will also want to find ways for faculty to document their participation in these professional development activities. Documentation via a certificate of completion can be especially helpful to part-time faculty who can include this on their resume. It can also be used in the reappointment, tenure, and promotion processes.

Consultation and Mentoring Services

In addition to professional development events, many Teaching and Learning Centers offer one-on-one consulting or mentoring services. Individual consultation is the second most frequently offered service after workshops (Beach et al., 2016). An advantage of the one-on-one consultation is that it provides faculty with individualized support and resources.

Although this approach can tax a Teaching and Learning Center with limited resources, it can be extremely beneficial to faculty. Faculty will appreciate the opportunity to discuss the culture and structure of their learning environments to identify teaching strategies that are contextualized to their setting. This individualized approach allow for these conversations to take place.

Mentoring programs are also a frequently offered service provided by Teaching and Learning Centers. New faculty mentoring programs are the most common types of mentoring provided. In a new faculty mentoring program, new faculty who want to participate are provided with one or two mentors.

The multiple mentor approach is advantageous for several reasons. First, it provides new faculty with several perspectives. Second, because one mentor is often outside of the faculty member's department, it can sometimes be easier for the new faculty member to candidly share challenges without fear this will have a negative impact on their daily interactions in the department. In addition, having multiple mentors increases the likelihood that new faculty will have mentors from the same gender and/or race.

Mentoring programs have been shown to be effective. Thurston, Navarrete, and Miller (2009), for instance, evaluated a new faculty mentoring program that was in place for ten years and found it was successful from the administrator, mentor, and mentee perspective. One important finding was that the mentoring program contributed to a culture of collaboration. Hanover Research (2014) indicates the following best practices for faculty mentoring programs:

- Mentoring program is supported by senior administrators.
- Mentoring is embedded in other professional development programming.
- Mentoring is voluntary.
- Mentoring training and support are provided.
- Mentoring is assessed.

CONCLUDING REMARKS

Colleges that are establishing or enhancing a Teaching and Learning Center should be commended for making teaching and learning a priority. The Teaching and Learning Center director and staff members can serve as change agents by facilitating improvements in teaching and learning practices which will undoubtedly improve student success outcomes.

Colleges launching a new Center will need to consider the structure for leadership and who will best be able to lead this effort. After a leadership team is established, the focus will need to shift to formulating, communicating, and enacting the vision and mission of the Teaching and Learning Center. Throughout this process, Teaching and Learning Center leaders will want to determine how the Center can best support institutional goals and priorities related to teaching and learning. Teaching and Learning Centers can provide faculty with support through a variety of programs and services including workshops, faculty learning communities, and individual consultation and mentoring. These efforts directly tap into the ensuring learning essential practice of guided pathways and will positively impact student success.

Chapter Two

Program and Course Learning Outcomes and Assessment

At the end of this chapter, you will be able to:

1. Describe strategies that can be used to engage faculty in assessment.
2. Determine institutional strategies that communicate the importance of assessment.
3. Identify a professional development plan to support faculty with assessment.

Conversations about student success are taking place on every college campus. Student success is often the theme of mission statements and strategic plans. However, defining success can be a complicated task. Some of the most commonly used metrics to measure student success are persistence or retention rates and graduation rates. These statistics are fairly easy to track and can shed some light on whether colleges are achieving their goals related to student success.

Retention and graduation statistics alone do not tell the complete story about student success. Of particular importance, these statistics do not provide much information about student learning. In addition to determining if students are making it to the finish line, colleges need to account for how much learning has taken place along this journey. Instead of relying solely on traditional outcome measures such as graduation and retention, colleges and universities also need to assess student learning at the course and program level.

Accountability is important. In recent years, accrediting bodies have been placing increased emphasis on assessment practices. Assessment of learning is a priority focus area for all seven accrediting bodies, and, as a result, colleges and universities across the nation are placing a high priority on student learning (Gannon-Slater, Ikenberry, Jankowski, & Kuh, 2014). More specifically, accrediting bodies require colleges to continually and actively engage in assessment to determine whether students are in fact absorbing the knowledge and skills identified as learning outcomes for the various programs offered.

In addition, and perhaps more importantly, colleges are expected to use assessment data as a tool for improvement. Suskie (2018) notes that there is little to no value in assessment processes if teaching and learning are not improved as a result of engaging in assessment. Colleges therefore need to make improvements and changes based on assessment data.

Fortunately, accrediting bodies are now requiring more than the act of conducting assessment data. In the early years of assessment being a requirement of accrediting bodies, colleges were expected to have assessment plans in place. The bar has since been raised.

Today, colleges must demonstrate that they continually engage in assessment. They also must use assessment data to guide decisions and actions aimed at improving student learning. In addition, they need to measure the success of these efforts and the level of progress made in terms of improving student learning. This is often referred to as closing the loop.

According to findings from a 2013 national survey conducted by the National Institute for Learning Outcomes Assessment (NILOA), chief academic officers reported high levels of responsiveness to standards set by accrediting bodies (Gannon-Slater et al., 2014). Thus, when accrediting bodies make the use of assessment a priority, colleges respond and engage in these actions. It is therefore fortunate that accrediting bodies have stepped up their expectations regarding the use of assessment to improve learning.

The process of learning outcomes assessment involves the following steps:

1. Determine learning outcomes.
2. Develop assessment plans.
3. Collect data.
4. Analyze data and determine what improvement actions are needed.
5. Engage in improvement actions.
6. Reassess to determine if improvement actions are resulting in the desired effect of increased student learning.

Although assessment is becoming a much more familiar and valued process on campuses across the nation, many faculty are not engaged in such practices on a regular basis. In fact, many faculty view assessment as an administrative task rather than one that is directly connected to teaching and learning. Hutchings (2010) notes that increased faculty engagement is a consistent desire of high-level administrators and the value of faculty in assessment is widely recognized, yet colleges and universities have not been successful at engaging faculty in meaningful ways.

Several obstacles to faculty engagement exist. For example, faculty are often not provided with training on the value of assessment or how to effectively engage in program- and course-level assessment. Faculty, especially at community colleges, have incredibly heavy teaching loads which makes time for assessment a challenge.

This issue of time and workload is one that is consistently identified as a challenge by faculty from a range of disciplines at various institutions (McCullough & Jones, 2014). Furthermore, the institutional reward processes have not elevated assessment to a place of high enough importance to make it a priority for faculty (Hutchings, 2010). In some cases, especially for part-time faculty, the reward structure may even be nonexistent.

The lack of faculty engagement in assessment is unfortunate because assessment influences student learning and is an activity that needs to be led by the faculty. Faculty know what students should be learning and thus can develop meaningful program and course learning outcomes. Faculty are also constantly designing assessments for use in their classes to determine whether students have achieved the learning goals for the course.

As a result, faculty have the background and expertise needed to engage in course- and program-level assessment. Colleges need to capitalize on this and involve full and part-time faculty in assessment. Teaching and Learning Centers can be a great resource for this work.

MAKING THE CASE FOR FACULTY ENGAGEMENT IN ASSESSMENT

Prior to asking faculty to engage in assessment activities, it is critical for institutions to set the stage by sharing the value and purpose of assessment. As discussed in a recent report from the Community College Research Center (CCRC), when colleges spend a significant amount of time on case-making and planning before jumping into action and implementation, this leads to successful outcomes for students (Jenkins, Lahr, Brown, & Mazzariello, 2019). Explaining the rationale for assessment is therefore critical.

Colleges are likely feeling pressure from accrediting bodies to do more and do it quickly when it comes to assessment. Despite these pressures, colleges need to first spend time and energy on educating and engaging the campus community and other key stakeholders about the value of assessment and the essential role of faculty in assessment. Skipping this important part of the process can result in negative attitudes and a lack of participation in assessment efforts.

Making the case needs to address misconceptions about who is responsible for assessment. Assessment is often viewed as an administrative task and responsibility (Hutchings, 2010). Assessment was not initially a part of a faculty member's responsibilities if they were hired prior to assessment being made a priority by accrediting bodies. Even today, many faculty job descriptions do not emphasize or even include assessment. Thus, it is not surprising that faculty would not view assessment as one of their responsibilities.

In addition, making the case efforts need to address the dual purposes of assessment. Penn (2007) articulately described these dual purposes as "assessment for them" and "assessment for us." He notes that accountability assessment or "assessment for them" focuses on providing external constituents such as legislators, parents, and the community at large with information about retention and completion rates. "Assessment for us" focuses on exploring the processes and outcomes of teaching and learning and looking for ways to improve practices that increase student learning.

Another way to describe the two different purposes of assessments is "prove it" and "improve it." Calls for accountability require colleges to measure and report standardized outcome measures such as graduation and retention. In essence, colleges are being asked to demonstrate or prove effectiveness with high retention and graduation rates. This can be referred to as "prove it" assessment.

"Improve it" assessment processes, on the other hand, look more closely at the methods and outcomes along the way so the data can be used for improvement. Fortunately, colleges can do both when they lead with an improvement focus. Engaging in "improve it" assessment leads to increased learning, and, as a result, "prove it" data points such as retention and graduation rates will also improve.

Not surprisingly, faculty are often less interested in "assessment for them" (Penn, 2007) as this is perceived as a task for institutional effectiveness administrators. Unfortunately, most faculty view assessment in this way. In a recent survey of more than 2,000 instructors and 200 leaders conducted by Inside Higher Ed, 59% of the faculty who responded stated they agreed with the following statement: "Assessment efforts seem primarily focused on satisfying outside groups such as accreditors or politicians, rather than serving students" (Lederman, 2018a). This perception of assessment will serve as an obstacle to faculty engagement.

Colleges need to more heavily emphasize the "assessment for us" or "improve it" process of assessment and illustrate to faculty and other professionals on campus how these dual purposes of assessment are connected. Explicitly connecting assessment processes to teaching processes is needed. Faculty may not immediately recognize how assessment is connected to their daily work, especially since assessment requirements initially came from external bodies rather than stemming from teaching and learning profession-als.

Helping faculty see how assessment can support their work with students in the classroom will get faculty interested and engaged in assessment. For example, colleges can share examples of how engaging in assessment led to improved academic performance for students. As with all tasks, motivation to participate in a task is higher when the value of the task is readily appar-ent.

When colleges engage in the "assessment for us" or "improve it" process of assessment, teaching and learning gain center-stage attention. As faculty discover problems related to classroom learning, they will naturally look for ways to make modifications aimed at improving student learning. Thus, en-gaging in assessment for improvement processes will likely lead to changes in teaching practices and, ultimately, improved student learning. These class-room-level changes and improvements in learning will undoubtedly have a positive impact on the "assessment for them" or "prove it" data.

Unfortunately, faculty say they have not seen how assessment efforts improve teaching and learning at the classroom level or increase graduation rates at the institutional level. In fact, Lederman (2018a) reports that more faculty disagree rather than agree with survey statements about assessment helping to improve the quality of teaching and learning or degree completion rates. This may be due to most of the faculty responses in this survey (52%) indicating they do not "regularly receive data gathered from their college's assessment efforts."

Colleges need to regularly share data that tell the assessment story so that faculty see the fruits of their assessment labor. Too often, assessment reports are filed away and not regularly used. Keeping assessment data visible and accessible to all members of the campus community, especially faculty, is critically important.

The Institutional Research Office is a key campus resource that can pro-vide training and package assessment data for faculty. Brief, visually effec-tive assessment documents need to be regularly shared with the campus community. Many colleges are using data dashboards to display key perfor-mance indicators (KPI) such as the number of students completing college-level English or math or earning at least fifteen credits by the end of the first semester or first year. Colleges need to ensure that faculty are aware of data dashboards and are trained in how to view, interpret, and use them.

At campus-wide meetings, it can be helpful to have a combination of administrators, faculty, and staff present on the value of assessment. When faculty talk passionately about why assessment matters, this can really reso-nate with other faculty members. Despite faculty engagement not being as high as it should be, there are still many faculty members who are engaged in this work and can be called upon to inspire others to do the same.

According to a recent survey of more than 2,000 faculty, 34% of the responders indicated they are using assessment data to improve teaching and learning (Lederman, 2018a). Colleges can tap into these faculty leaders for assistance with communicating the value and importance of assessment. Colleges need to not only consider the messages they want to share about assessment but also who can best communicate these messages.

DETERMINING INSTITUTIONAL STRATEGIES TO PRIORITIZE ASSESSMENT

Colleges and universities are faced with numerous tasks related to educating students so that they have the skills and knowledge needed to be productive citizens and successful in their careers. Prioritizing which tasks and initiatives are most important is a constant challenge because so many colleges and universities, especially community colleges, are underresourced (Mellow & Heelan, 2014). Determining what needs to be a priority can stem from internal processes such as strategic planning and external processes such as requirements set by accrediting bodies.

One of the most positive outcomes of the accreditation process is that colleges and universities must engage in assessment in order to maintain accreditation status. These external influences and requirements have definitely increased campus-wide assessment efforts at colleges and universities across the nation (McCullough & Jones, 2014). Colleges and universities must and do respond to the expectations and requirements for reaccreditation, which makes assessment a priority.

The prioritization of assessment also needs to stem from internal processes. It is imperative for faculty and staff from across the institution to converse about the value of assessment. As one would expect, faculty and staff will be more committed to an activity when they see the purpose and value, and when they are a part of the decision to make it a priority.

A bottom-up or inside-out approach, as opposed to a top-down or outside-in approach, leads to high levels of investment and engagement in the process. An excellent place for assessment to be explicitly communicated is in the strategic plan. Institutions can emphasize the significant role assessment plays in teaching and learning by making it visible in key documents.

If the strategic planning process results in a focus on assessment, then the budget should also convey the importance of assessment. In a recent keynote address, Pando (2019) emphasized how budgets communicate institutional priorities. Thus, if assessment is an institutional priority, there should be evidence of this in the budget.

For example, the college may provide release time or a stipend to faculty who are leading assessment efforts. In addition, funds for professional development and assessment tools would likely be incorporated into the budget. McCullough and Jones (2014) found that colleges that provided financial support for conferences and the purchasing of assessment tools were more likely to have higher levels of faculty engagement with assessment.

Reward structures provide an avenue to communicate priorities to faculty. One of the most significant reward structures is the tenure and promotion process. Hutchings (2010) notes that assessment "has often been undervalued or invisible in promotion and tenure deliberations, a circumstance that has certainly not encouraged faculty to see assessment as their work" (p. 9).

Incorporating assessment as a primary area of focus in the evaluation process would undoubtedly communicate to faculty that assessment needs to be a priority. Colleges and universities that are serious about increasing faculty participation in assessment need to reevaluate current processes for tenure and promotion. Modifications will likely be needed so that assessment is included in these evaluation processes.

Because it can be quite challenging and time-consuming for change to occur with long-standing processes such as tenure and promotion, colleges and universities will also want to find other ways to bring attention to assessment in the present. Recognition for assessment work can also increase the visibility and importance of assessment. For example, adding an Assessment Award for faculty and staff who have engaged in assessment and made changes that resulted in increased learning is an excellent way to highlight the importance of assessment.

Another example could be to showcase success stories. For example, colleges and universities could share assessment stories in newsletters or other publications. Stories can serve as models and inspiration.

The job description is another important document that can be used to convey assessment as a priority. When hiring new faculty or staff, it is important for colleges to emphasize assessment in job descriptions. This clearly communicates that assessment is a priority and that assessment is a part of faculty and staff responsibilities.

College administrators can also have conversations with the office of human resources and faculty unions, if applicable, about modifying job descriptions or contracts to include assessment as a requirement. Assessment questions can also be incorporated into the application and interview process for faculty positions. Keeping assessment visible from the start will help change the culture about assessment on campus.

PROVIDING ASSESSMENT-FOCUSED
PROFESSIONAL DEVELOPMENT

The lack of training or professional development is another key obstacle to faculty involvement in assessment. Hutchings (2010) notes that assessment is not typically a part of one's graduate training and that opportunities for faculty to learn about assessment are often limited. The more confidence one has in their ability to complete a task, the more likely it is they will pursue this task. Not surprising, faculty who have not been trained on how to do assessment will not be inclined to seek out assessment opportunities.

Professional development can build faculty confidence and interest in assessment and this will likely result in higher levels of participation. Faculty training needs to focus on understanding the process and value of assessment. Training sessions can address how to determine program and course learning outcomes, how to identify assessment tools that will provide evidence on whether outcomes were achieved, and strategies to use assessment data to improve student learning. Assessment offices and Teaching and Learning Centers can be helpful resources as colleges move this work forward.

Determining Program and Course Learning Outcomes

Assessment-focused professional development needs to begin by assisting faculty with identifying learning outcomes. Backward design principles and processes can be used to assist faculty with understanding the assessment process. It can be a helpful framework that illustrates the importance of first articulating outcomes. According to Wiggins and McTighe (2005), the backward design process involves the following three steps:

1. Determine the desired goals or outcomes.
2. Determine what assessment would provide evidence of the successful achievement of the outcomes.
3. Determine how to best teach and support students so they will perform successfully on the assessments, demonstrating the achievement of learning outcomes.

Starting this process at the program level encourages faculty and administrators to think carefully about the overall goals and outcomes. Thus, the first step in this process is to determine or reevaluate program learning outcomes. Program learning outcomes explicitly communicate what graduates of a program or major will know, think, or do (Suskie, 2018).

Helping faculty identify program-level learning outcomes as opportunities to communicate the purpose of their program, and corresponding knowledge and skills students will possess upon graduation, can increase faculty engagement in this process. Faculty tend to be very interested in having conversations about and bringing attention to the goals of learning. Sharing the learning outcomes on websites, on syllabi, and verbally with students are excellent options to help students see the value and purpose of their degree program.

Determining the overall goals of a program can be a relatively easy task for faculty. However, the challenge for faculty is often articulating these goals using measurable language. Using measurable language is critical because if this type of language is not used, it will be impossible to determine if the outcomes were achieved (Suskie, 2018).

To assist faculty with developing or revising measurable program learning outcomes, professional development can emphasize Bloom's (1956) taxonomy. According to Bloom's taxonomy revised by Anderson and Krathwohl (2001), there are different levels of knowing. In this hierarchical model, lower levels of knowing must take place before students will be able to engage in higher levels of learning.

The levels of learning associated with this taxonomy, from lowest to highest, are remembering, understanding, applying, evaluating, and creating (Anderson & Krathwohl, 2001). This model will likely resonate with faculty. They understand the critical role of foundational knowledge needed prior to being able to effectively engage in higher-level cognitive tasks.

To support faculty, colleges can provide lists of action verbs associated with the various levels of knowing in Bloom's revised taxonomy (Anderson & Krathwohl, 2001). Action verbs such as *explain* or *evaluate* articulate the level of knowledge using measurable language. In addition, examples from other institutions or other programs within the same institution can be shared. These frameworks, resources, and examples will be useful to faculty.

It is crucial that program-level outcomes be revisited regularly to ensure they accurately represent the skills and competencies needed by graduates in the field. This is particularly noteworthy in rapidly changing industries. If a program has an advisory board, members can be asked to evaluate current outcomes to determine if they align with industry needs.

Part-time faculty can also be an asset in this process as many are employed full time in the field. Given their connection to the industry, part-time faculty can likely add tremendous value to the assessment conversations. They will often have firsthand knowledge of what graduates will need to comprehend in order to be successful in the workplace.

Once program-level outcomes have been established or revised, faculty should turn their attention to course-level outcomes. Course learning outcomes need to align with program-level learning outcomes. Faculty will need to determine how the courses in the program can be tailored to ensure students achieve the program learning outcomes identified.

In highly sequenced and cohort model programs, the connection between courses and the program learning outcomes can be clear and easy to articulate. This process can become more challenging in programs where there is extensive flexibility and choice surrounding course selection. For example, students majoring in liberal arts degrees can often choose from a large variety of courses.

Although colleges fully engaged in guided pathways will be identifying shorter lists of recommended options within each category, there will still be several degrees that have a significant amount of choice built into the curriculum. For community colleges with several four-year partners, the complexity of the transfer processes may require more choice in the curriculum. Faculty will need to consider why the courses are listed as options, how these courses can support student achievement of the program learning outcomes, and their transferability.

Mapping course and program learning outcomes can be a valuable activity for full and part-time faculty. Colleges can use mandatory meeting times to engage faculty in these discussions and can provide guidance and models on how to map course learning outcomes to the overall program learning outcomes. To engage in this process, faculty begin by listing the program learning outcomes as column headers in a table and all the required courses in the first column. Colleges can then determine what type of coding system to use in each cell of the table.

One approach is to simply put an X in the cell if there is a link between the course and program learning outcomes. However, this type of map would not provide information about how significant the connection is between the course and program. Another approach that colleges may opt to use is to ask faculty to make judgments about how much the course and program learning outcomes connect. Then, instead of an X in the cell, letters indicating the strength of the connection could be entered. For example, "L" could be used for limited connection, "M" for moderate connection, and "H" for high-level connection between the course and program outcome.

Establishing measurable course-level learning outcomes can ensure all faculty focus on the same learning goals. Agreeing on the core learning outcomes for a class can be a challenging task as faculty members will likely have different opinions about what matters most. Using the mapping process can assist faculty in determining what course-level outcomes best align with program-level outcomes.

It is also important for faculty to realize that the core learning outcomes do not prohibit a faculty member from addressing the outcomes in a manner that fits their pedagogical style or approach. Faculty can also add to the curriculum and address other topics and outcomes as time permits. It simply ensures the outcomes agreed upon by the department faculty are the primary areas of focus.

Program- and Course-Level Assessments

After the program- and course-level learning outcomes have been developed or revised, the next step is for faculty to determine how the outcomes will be assessed. Faculty are familiar with identifying assessments as they regularly use a variety of assessment tools in their courses. However, this process requires faculty to view assessment from a broader lens, identifying tools that will tell the story about whether graduates achieved the stated program outcomes and how students are achieving course outcomes across all sections of a course, not just in their course.

Bringing full and part-time faculty who teach the same subject together for a conversation about program- and course-level assessment is a powerful strategy. During department meetings, faculty can share ideas about what types of assessments will show evidence of students having achieved the program- and course-level learning outcomes. Some examples at the program level might be a comprehensive exam, capstone experience, paper, or culminating project.

Colleges may opt to purchase assessment tools that have been already developed and used at colleges across the nation. The benefit of using already established assessments is that colleges can start using these immediately. However, the cost may be problematic, and the assessments may not provide the specific information needed.

Fortunately, the Association of American Colleges and Universities engaged faculty and other professionals in education from various types of institutions across the nation and developed VALUE (Valid Assessment of Learning in Undergraduate Education) rubrics on core general education outcomes that can be used by institutions at no cost (Rhodes, 2010). The following rubrics were created and have been widely used at colleges and universities across the nation:

- Inquiry and analysis
- Critical thinking
- Creative thinking
- Written communication
- Oral communication
- Quantitative literacy
- Information literacy
- Reading
- Teamwork
- Problem-solving
- Civic knowledge and engagement—local and global
- Intercultural knowledge and competence
- Ethical reasoning and action

- Global learning
- Foundations and skills for lifelong learning
- Integrative learning (Rhodes, 2010)

Since the release of VALUE rubrics in 2009, reliability and validity has been investigated and demonstrated (McConnell & Rhodes, 2017). These faculty-developed tools have been used to show student performance and identify areas where continued growth is needed. Thus, the impressive set of VALUE rubrics can be used by institutions with confidence for program assessment.

Another option is for colleges to develop homegrown assessment tools that align well with the program outcomes. This approach can be quite time-consuming. However, it may result in an assessment that directly matches the outcomes defined by the institution and be particularly useful when assessing more specific program outcomes.

Perhaps the greatest challenge with program-level assessment is not just determining the assessment tool but determining how this data will be collected. This is particularly challenging when a program does not require a capstone course or lacks a clear sequential pattern to the coursework. In this situation, there is not an easy way to assess students at the time of graduation.

Some colleges have opted for a graduation assessment. Colleges using this approach ask students to complete an assessment when they apply for graduation. The challenge, of course, is that colleges do not want to put up unnecessary gates that might deter a student from graduating. Another approach that colleges have used is to gather sample assignments from various courses to show growth from courses taken early in the program as compared to courses taken toward the end of the program.

Faculty need to be active participants in these conversations. Faculty expertise is needed to determine if a capstone experience needs to be added to the curriculum and what type of assessment would best assess program outcomes. However, it is important to note that decisions need to be made collaboratively at the institutional level.

Although the assessment of program learning outcomes needs to take center stage in the program assessment process, it is likely that colleges will also want to gather additional data about the program during the assessment process. For example, colleges may want to know the student enrollment by program, success rates in required courses, percentage of students graduating, transfer rates, and employment statistics upon graduation.

After program-level assessment tools and processes have been determined, faculty will then need to focus on course-level assessment. Although faculty are probably using effective assessment tools in their classes, course-level assessment requires consistent use of tools across all sections of a course. Thus, faculty will need to discuss which assessment tools best capture the course-level assessment data needed and agree to use these tools across all sections.

It is best for assessments to be incorporated into current class practices. This way, the course- or program-level assessment does not become an additional task for faculty or students but rather one that is part of the coursework. For example, using a consistent assessment tool such as the final exam, or perhaps common items on an exam, in all sections of a course does not require additional work by faculty as the exam would already likely be one of the course assignments. Another example is to have a consistent final project that is used across sections.

Using Assessment Data for Improvement

Improvement plans and actions cannot be put into place until after faculty carefully review assessment data. Unfortunately, faculty often report not having access to assessment data (Lederman, 2018a). Faculty want to see institutional-level data and are also interested in learning how the performance of their students compares with students at other institutions.

The lack of comparative data from other institutions is an area that faculty find frustrating (McCullough & Jones, 2014). Thus, colleges need to consistently share institutional and comparative data in meaningful and user-friendly formats with faculty. Data can serve as a vehicle to start meaningful conversations about teaching and learning.

McConnell and Rhodes (2017) argue that assessment data can also play an important role in equity conversations. They noted that only 17% of chief academic officers responding to a survey indicated that their college or university disaggregated data on "student achievement of learning outcomes by such critical factors as race and ethnicity, socioeconomic status, and parents' level of educational attainment" (p. 49). They urged colleges and universities to not only use data to broadly look at student performance but to also investigate and address equity gaps.

Colleges need to identify opportunities for faculty and administrators to engage in a meaningful review of the data. Scheduling regular meetings throughout the academic year designated specifically for program review and having assessment as a standing agenda item at department meetings are strategies that some colleges use. These are great ways to ensure assessment processes occur regularly at colleges.

Packaging data in user-friendly documents is helpful. Data can be complex, and charts or graphs that make sense to those who created them may not be easy for others to interpret. Faculty can find it frustrating to receive data that is difficult to understand and interpret. It is, therefore, a good idea for colleges to lean on institutional research offices to create infographics or executive summaries that will be easy for faculty to understand and use.

Colleges can provide guidance and examples of how assessment data has been used to inform decision-making. At the program level, a review of assessment data may lead faculty and administrators to determine some programs need to be modified, retired, or created. It is important to acknowledge that program assessment may illuminate the need to retire programs that are no longer responding to the demands in the field. This is understandably one of the reasons why faculty can be reluctant to engage in this process.

Assessment is about improvement, and, in most cases, engaging in this process will lead faculty to discover ways to improve and build upon existing programs. However, there may be a few situations where colleges can better serve students by retiring a program and refocusing faculty time and energy on improving other existing programs or developing a new program that can respond to the current workforce. Decisions to retire programs or create new ones should only be made after careful consideration of all available data.

It can be challenging to determine how to improve programs. One of the best ways to assist full and part-time faculty with this process is by giving faculty opportunities to engage in meaningful conversations about assessment data. Having these conversations with colleagues from different institutions can add value because different perspectives and ideas are more likely.

Unfortunately, cross-institution conversations on assessment and teaching and learning are not common. These cross-institution dialogues can be particularly important in departments that are very small. In fact, some community colleges may only have one or two faculty members teaching a discipline. Working with those doing similar work at other institutions can help faculty see beyond current institutional practices and explore different approaches that can lead to improved teaching and learning on their own campus.

College administrators can support cross-institutional, discipline-specific meetings by hosting events on their campus and providing refreshments for participants. These meetings can be face-to-face, but with the numerous technology tools available, online platforms are also viable options. Online meetings may enable more significant participation.

Although focusing on improvement is obviously the major point of engaging in assessment, it is important to note that assessment can also shed light on what is working well. When faculty discover what approaches are working well, they should be empowered to share these strategies with colleagues at their own institution and with colleagues from other institutions. This can happen via informal presentations or conversations, formal presentations at conferences, and various publication outlets. Showcasing what is working can help others also make improvements in an effort to support student learning.

CONCLUDING REMARKS

It is essential that colleges assess student learning to determine if learning goals were achieved. Assessment needs to happen at the program and course level and faculty expertise and participation is critical. Colleges need to make the case for assessment and show faculty the value of engaging in assessment processes for the purpose of improving student learning.

Colleges will also need to provide training and support to faculty. Training can focus on topics such as developing outcomes, determining assessment tools, and, most importantly, using assessment data to improve teaching and learning practices. Communicating assessment data and sharing success stories across the campus is important.

Chapter Three

Backward Course Design

At the end of this chapter, you will be able to:

1. Describe backward design and how course design impacts student learning.
2. Determine strategies to train and support faculty in backward design.

The student's experience in the classroom plays a significant role in their ultimate success. Colleges committed to improving student success outcomes will need to focus their attention on the teaching and learning practices taking place in the classroom. The classroom is where students spend most of their time while attending college, especially at community colleges. Students taking fifteen credits per semester spend approximately 450 hours in the classroom each year. Thus, the classroom is the place where the greatest impact on student success can be made.

Fortunately, some colleges engaged in guided pathways are turning their attention to the classroom. Valencia College in Florida is one example. At a recent national conference on student success, Shugart (2018) shared institutional data from Valencia College that showed the importance of students successfully completing early courses.

Students who attempted at least five courses during their first academic year and were successful in all five of these courses had a fall-to-fall retention rate of 86.3%, but if a student did not pass just one of these five courses, the fall-to-fall retention rate dropped to 73.3% (Shugart, 2018). This retention rate dropped even further to 57.3% for those who were only successful in three of the five courses and to 34.6% for those who were successful in less than three courses.

Shugart also shared data that showed performance in the first five courses has a long-term impact on success. The five-year graduation rate for full-time students who successfully completed five courses in their first academic year was 60.4% while this rate significantly dropped for those who only successfully completed four courses (34.7%), three courses (20.7%), and less than three courses (7.3%). These findings illustrate that the student learning experience in the classroom is an incredibly important area of focus for colleges engaged in the guided pathways movement.

Improving teaching is one of the most powerful ways to improve student outcomes. Research studies have shown that effective instruction is linked to better student outcomes (Brown & Kurzweil, 2018). Although faculty regularly reflect on their teaching practices and as a result make adjustments aimed at improving student learning, they are often doing so without much guidance or support from the institution. In essence, revising teaching practices is often a trial-and-error process.

One of the most effective ways to assist faculty with improving their teaching is by providing faculty with professional development regarding effective course design. Research has found that student performance improves when faculty participate in professional development targeting course design and then redesign their courses using these principles (Swan, Matthews, Bogle, Boles, & Day, 2012). In addition to improved academic performance, students also report higher levels of engagement and satisfaction with courses designed well (Armbruster, Patel, Johnson, & Weiss, 2009; Reynolds & Kearns, 2017).

COURSE DESIGN FRAMEWORKS

Wiggins and McTighe (2005) describe three course design frameworks: content or coverage-based design, activity-based design, and backward design. Content or coverage-based design and activity-based design are very commonly used approaches, but these approaches will not likely result in the highest level of learning for students. Backward design, on the other hand, is connected to increased student performance and experiences.

Content or Coverage-based Design

Content or coverage-based design is the approach most faculty are using. In this approach, faculty first identify a list of content areas or topics that need to be covered in the class and then they design the course around these content areas. Thus, as the name of this approach implies, the coverage-based approach focuses on making sure all the topics are covered or taught.

Many faculty, especially those who are new to teaching, may rely on a textbook to provide the list of content and then design the course around the textbook being used for the class. To facilitate this process, textbook publishers have created textbooks with fifteen chapters to align to the fifteen weeks in the semester. Thus, the organization of textbooks makes it easy and convenient for faculty to use the coverage-based design approach.

Although this approach can ensure the identified topics are covered, it does not necessarily guarantee that students will achieve the learning outcomes of the course. Because learning outcomes in this approach are not the focus, the successful achievement of learning outcomes is left to chance. Learning outcomes targeting skill development, in particular, will not likely be a focus in the coverage or content-based approach.

Activity-based Design

Many faculty also use activity-based design. In an activity-based course design approach, the focus is on the learning activities. Faculty using this approach have a high interest in engaging students in the learning process. When faculty use this framework to design their courses, a new or engaging teaching strategy will take center stage in the course design process. For example, the faculty member may design the course so that clickers or polling tools are used on a daily basis or ensure group activities take place during every class.

Although this approach is well-intended because it is focused on student engagement and there is a significant body of research that supports the connection between student engagement and success (McClenney, 2007), the activity-based approach to course design also leaves the accomplishment of learning outcomes to chance. Skill development may be more likely, depending on the teaching strategies used, but content may not be fully addressed. As a result, students may leave the course without the identified knowledge needed to be successful in subsequent courses and in their career field.

Backward Design

Backward design is the most effective approach to course design. According to Wiggins and McTighe (2005), backward design can be defined as designing with the end in mind. Faculty using backward design need to first focus on the learning outcomes and then use these learning outcomes to drive the design process. Backward design involves three steps:

1. Determining the course learning outcomes.
2. Identifying assessments that will provide evidence of student achievement of the learning outcomes.
3. Determining which teaching methods will best support student achievement of the learning outcomes.

Determining Learning Outcomes

The first step involves carefully considering the goals of the course. In higher education, the goals of the course are referred to as course learning outcomes. Course learning outcomes clearly describe what students will know, think, or do as a result of successfully completing the course. Learning outcomes need to be stated in measurable terms.

Bloom's taxonomy is often used as a guide when developing learning outcomes (Betts, 2008). Using Bloom's taxonomy is helpful because it requires faculty to think about what level of knowing or understanding is needed. In the most recently revised version of Bloom's taxonomy (Anderson & Krathwohl, 2001), the following levels of knowing were identified:

- remembering
- understanding
- applying
- analyzing
- evaluating
- creating

Some courses, especially introductory ones, will likely include lower-level cognitive goals such as being able to remember or recall essential facts and concepts related to the discipline. However, college courses need to go beyond the foundational skill of remembering. More advanced skills such as being able to apply concepts, compare and contrast concepts, and analyze and evaluate concepts are also needed.

The more advanced the course, the more likely the outcomes will be focused on the development of cognitively complex skills. When faculty use Bloom's taxonomy as a guide to develop course learning outcomes, more attention will be given to the various levels of cognitive skills that need to be developed or mastered in each course. Clearly articulated and measurable learning outcomes drive the design process.

Resources that provide sample action verbs related to Bloom's taxonomy will be helpful to faculty. Using action verbs aligned to Bloom's taxonomy enables faculty to think more clearly about their expectations and helps them state the course learning outcomes in measurable terms. Using measurable language is very important as it is impossible to determine if outcomes were achieved if they were not defined in measurable terms.

Colleges will want to engage both full and part-time faculty in the process of identifying, reviewing, and revising learning outcomes. Professional development focused on how to determine and evaluate learning outcomes will also be important. Colleges can utilize campus professionals with expertise in assessment and teaching and learning to provide training or bring in outside experts from neighboring institutions.

To make learning outcomes training accessible to all faculty, including part-time faculty who are often left out of the conversation, sessions can be live-streamed or recorded, or experts can develop online modules accessible via a learning management system. Resources such as action verb lists associated with Bloom's taxonomy (Anderson & Krathwohl, 2001) and sample learning outcomes for different disciplines can be placed online. It is critical that all faculty are included in these important conversations.

Emphasizing learning outcomes at department and institutional meetings is an excellent way to pave the way for backward design. Faculty can be encouraged to regularly ask colleagues about how assessments and teaching strategies being used connect back to learning outcomes. Keeping learning outcomes visible and using outcomes to guide decision-making will lead to improved course design and increased student learning.

Learning outcomes also need to be communicated to students. Faculty can be encouraged to share and discuss learning outcomes with their students not only at the start of the semester but also throughout the semester when those particular outcomes are being addressed. Learning outcomes should be prominently placed at the beginning of the syllabus and visual strategies such as bold, color, or larger font can be used to bring attention to them (Harrington & Thomas, 2018). These strategies can send the message to students that learning outcomes are critically important and are driving the design of the course.

Identifying Assessments

The second step in the backward design process is identifying assessments that will provide evidence that the learning outcomes were successfully achieved. This involves determining what types of summative assessments will best tell the story about whether students have achieved the course-level learning outcomes. Formative assessments that provide information about whether students are on track to successfully complete the summative assessments will then need to be identified.

Summative assessments are typically given at the end of the semester or unit as this type of assessment provides evidence of the achievement of learning outcomes. Formative assessments, on the other hand, are typically given throughout the semester as this type of assessment is designed to provide feedback on student progress of learning (Wininger, 2005). Examples of summative assessments include exams, papers, presentations, and projects. Quizzes and drafts are examples of formative assessment tools.

For existing courses that faculty have taught, faculty have already identified course assessments. However, engaging in backward design requires faculty to review assessment processes with a fresh perspective. Stepping back and reflecting on how the current assessments can be updated or revised is an important part of the process.

This can be quite challenging as it is likely faculty will believe the assignments or assessments they are currently using work well. Otherwise, they wouldn't be assigning these learning tasks. It is important to note that the current assessments may, of course, be valuable ways to determine if students have achieved the learning outcomes for the course. However, the current assessments may not be the only way to assess the learning outcomes and may not be the best option.

When engaging faculty in the backward design or redesign process, it can be helpful to encourage faculty to identify one or two major projects or assignments that can provide evidence whether students have successfully achieved the learning outcomes. In many cases, one well-crafted project or assignment can often provide evidence of multiple course learning outcomes. This is highly desirable because it means that student time and energy can be focused on these very meaningful tasks rather than having their attention and focus split between numerous less meaningful tasks.

Deeper levels of learning, often associated with higher levels of Bloom's taxonomy, are also more likely with more substantial learning tasks. Blessing and Blessing (2010), for instance, found that critical thinking skill development was more likely with a semester-long research project. Engaging in this process can help faculty think about which summative assessments will be of the most value.

The measurable language used in the learning outcomes will provide guidance on the type of assessment used to determine if the learning outcomes were achieved. As an example, if a psychology course has a learning outcome such as students will be able to establish action plans for individuals with different psychological disorders, this would be difficult to assess with an exam comprised of multiple-choice questions. A project-based assignment would better align with this learning outcome.

However, a learning outcome such as students will be able to apply classical and operant conditioning principles to an educational setting could potentially be assessed with multiple-choice questions that were carefully crafted to target these higher-level cognitive skills. It could also be assessed through written or oral assignments. The verb stem used in the learning outcomes illustrates the level of learning targeted and therefore needs to be used when determining appropriate assessments.

An excellent strategy to help faculty determine the best summative assessments is to encourage faculty to work with colleagues teaching the same course from within and outside their institution. Hosting cross-institution meetings for different disciplines or reserving time for internal discussions among colleagues teaching the same course provides the space and time for faculty to engage in meaningful conversations about backward design and assessment tools.

It is likely that various faculty members have approached the course somewhat differently and talking about the course goals and the value of various assignments can get creative ideas flowing. During these conversations, faculty may opt to select one or two of the assignments they were already using, perhaps with some minor modifications needed. However, faculty may also decide a different assessment will work better.

Together, faculty can develop a new signature project that aligns nicely with most, if not all, of the learning outcomes. This signature project can then be used across all sections of the course. These collaborative conversations will undoubtedly help faculty see various perspectives and identify the best assessment tools for the learning outcomes identified.

In addition to summative assessments, faculty will need to determine what types of formative assessment will work best in the course. Formative assessments are briefer assessments that provide information to both the student and faculty about whether the student is on track to perform well on the summative assessment. In other words, formative assessments provide valuable feedback to students about their progress toward the course learning outcomes that will be measured by the summative assessment.

Incorporating numerous formative assessment opportunities for students throughout the semester is recommended. Feedback is one of the most powerful learning tools (Nicol & Macfarlane-Dick, 2006). High levels of achievement are more likely when students have an opportunity to learn from successes and mistakes along the way. Formative assessments can, therefore, pave the way for student success.

There are many different types of formative assessments. One of the most common formative assessments is the quiz, which provides valuable feedback to students about whether they are on track to perform well on an exam. Online tools available via textbook publishers and within learning management systems make it easy for faculty to incorporate quizzes as a formative assessment tool. Online quizzes can be auto-graded so that students receive feedback immediately and faculty do not need to grade hundreds of quizzes each semester.

Another commonly used formative assessment technique is the draft. Prior to submitting a final paper or project, faculty can require students to submit an outline, a list of their sources, or a rough draft. Faculty teaching English often rely on this approach; however, faculty teaching other disciplines can also use drafts as a formative assessment tool. It can be incredibly time-consuming to grade multiple drafts so faculty will likely welcome strategies that can maximize the use of their time while still providing valuable feedback to students.

One approach is to only provide feedback on one aspect of the project such as whether the sources identified are appropriate to the assignment. Another approach is to use class time to have brief individual or group conferences with students while they are working on projects. When students receive feedback on these formative assessments, they will know if they are on the right track or if they will need to seek further support and assistance in order to meet with success on the summative assessment.

Formative assessments can also be valuable to faculty because the process can guide teaching. When faculty discover students are struggling with a task, more class time can be devoted to helping students develop the skill needed. In addition, these early indicators which show that a student is struggling can be shared via early alert systems so that student services professionals can reach out to students who may benefit from services such as tutoring.

By providing additional support as needed throughout the semester, faculty will increase the likelihood that students will perform well on the summative assessment. Grading quality work at the end of the semester is an incredibly rewarding experience for faculty. Students will also enjoy the experience of being successful.

It's a win-win for everyone. Students will learn more and be more successful and faculty will find this to be rewarding and inspirational. Colleges can emphasize these benefits at the start of department meetings or professional development programs.

Teaching Methods

After the learning outcomes and related assessments have been identified, the next and final step in backward design is for faculty to determine which teaching methods will best support student achievement of the learning outcomes. This is the part of the process that is likely of most interest to faculty, but it is very important that faculty do not jump ahead to this step until outcomes and assessments have been identified.

Working through the backward design process requires faculty to think critically about outcomes and assessment before turning their attention to teaching methods. This strategic process ensures that teaching methods align with the identified learning outcomes and will support student success on the associated summative assessments. Carefully working through the steps of backward design sequentially is important.

To determine which teaching method will work best, faculty need to think about what knowledge and skills students need in order to perform well on the summative projects. For example, if foundational knowledge is needed, lecturing might be the best teaching method. However, if students need to develop effective collaboration skills, a lecture will not likely lead to the best performance on the summative assessment. Instead, structured group work may be a better choice.

In most cases, a variety of teaching methods will need to be used in order to help students achieve the learning outcomes and perform well on the major summative assessments. The key here is to be thoughtful about which teaching method will produce the desired results. Engaging in this reflective backward design process will result in a well-organized course structure where outcomes, assessments, and teaching methods are aligned.

The backward course design process is an incredibly taxing process. It takes significant time, energy, effort, and reflection to effectively engage in this process and design or redesign a course. However, engaging in backward design is arguably one of the most effective ways to positively impact student success.

Students in a course that has been designed using this process will undoubtedly benefit. In a backward designed course, the course goals are clearly identified and the path to successfully achieving these goals are mapped out. In other words, a backward designed course provides students with a road map on how to achieve the course learning outcomes.

INSTITUTIONAL SUPPORT FOR BACKWARD DESIGN

Colleges can encourage and support faculty engagement in the backward design process by providing high-quality professional development on course design and giving faculty the time needed to explore this process. Because course design is a cognitively challenging task that requires significant focus and dedication, the timing of professional development is important. Rather than offering workshops and training during the semester when faculty attention is on current courses and students, a better solution may be to offer professional development at the conclusion of the spring semester. This way faculty can devote time during the summer months to design or redesign their courses. Faculty ready to work on sabbatical projects can also be encouraged to utilize this professional time for course design projects that can make a difference not only in their classrooms but can also be shared with others as a model and source of inspiration. The key is to provide faculty with support when they will be able to immediately apply what is learned.

Given the importance of the backward design process and the incredible amount of time and energy needed for this task, colleges may want to consider providing a financial incentive such as a stipend or course release if budgets allow. Reward structures communicate institutional priorities. Allocating funds to support faculty is an excellent way to illustrate the necessity of course design and can provide the incentive needed to engage more faculty in this process.

Faculty Learning Communities

Establishing a faculty learning community focused on the course design process is an excellent way to support faculty. Cox (2004) defines a faculty learning community as a "cross-disciplinary faculty and staff group of six to fifteen members (eight to twelve members is the recommended size) who engage in an active, collaborative, yearlong program with a curriculum about enhancing teaching and learning and with frequent seminars and activities that provide learning, development, the scholarship of teaching, and community building" (p. 8). In this case, the focus or topic area would be on backward design.

Research and assessment data provides strong evidence that faculty learning communities are effective (Cox, 2004). One of the reasons why a learning community is so valuable is because it provides faculty with an in-depth learning opportunity that parallels a graduate course experience. This approach goes well beyond many traditional professional development offerings that are only an hour or a day in duration.

Faculty learning communities also provide a structure for faculty colleagues to support and encourage one another as they take on challenging tasks such as course design. Participants often report that the cohort model used in learning communities fosters a supportive learning environment. Peer feedback on learning outcomes, assessments, and teaching methods can result in a well-thought-out and designed course. Benander (2013) strongly suggests that a peer-review process be incorporated into the faculty learning community and reports that faculty find this component of the program to be highly valuable.

In order to start a faculty learning community focused on course design, colleges will need to assess current resources, determine an assessment and implementation plan, and motivate and encourage faculty to participate. If a college has a Teaching and Learning Center, the director of the Center can take the lead on this project. Budgets will also need to be evaluated to determine if funds are available to provide a stipend or release time to facilitators and participants.

Collaboration between many different departments will be needed. Assessment professionals can help establish an assessment plan. Administrators will need to champion this new professional development opportunity to faculty.

The facilitator of the faculty learning community can develop the curriculum. It will be important for all members of the faculty learning community to have foundational background knowledge in backward design. After participants have developed a solid foundational knowledge in backward design, faculty can share experiences and progress with designing or re-designing their course. Colleagues can then ask questions to encourage reflective practices and can also provide suggestions and guidance.

Questioning

Another way to support faculty with learning about and implementing backward design is through questioning. Questioning is an excellent tool for reflection and is a great way to cognitively engage faculty in the course design task. Questions can be used to determine if goals are being accomplished. Wiggins and McTighe (2005), for example, suggest that faculty ask themselves the following questions when determining if assessments and outcomes align well:

- Can a student achieve the learning outcome but not do well on the major assessment?
- Can a student do well on the major assignment but not achieve the learning outcome?

Questions can also be used to help faculty develop the skills they need to effectively design the course. Instead of only providing information to faculty about backward design, it can be more helpful to engage faculty in conversations about the course design process. Carefully designed question prompts can be used to facilitate these meaningful conversations. When providing professional development on the first step in backward design—identifying learning outcomes—colleges may want to ask faculty the following questions:

- What do you want students to know, think, or do by the end of the course?
- What level of Bloom do your learning outcomes align to? How do lower and upper-level courses differ in terms of Bloom's taxonomy?
- What advanced cognitive skills do you want students to develop by the end of the semester?
- How can this course support the overall program learning outcomes?

Asking faculty questions that relate to step two of the backward design process—identifying assessments that align with learning outcomes—is also helpful. Questions can help faculty engage in reflection and think more deeply about teaching and learning. Sample questions that colleges can ask faculty about selecting assessments include:

- How do assignments relate to course and program outcomes as well as employer expectations?
- Which learning outcomes will this assessment measure?

- What other assessments or assignments might also demonstrate the achievement of the learning outcomes?
- How do the formative assessments support student achievement of the summative assessments? What skills or knowledge gaps might exist?
- What other formative assessment options would also work?

Finally, questions can also be helpful during the third and final step of the backward design process. Targeted questions on teaching methods will again require faculty to reflect on current practices and explore which teaching strategies will best support the learning goals. Sample questions focused on the third step of backward design, the teaching method, include:

- How do you know or will you know that the teaching methods you se-lected will help students achieve the course learning outcomes?
- What alternative teaching methods might also support the achievement of the learning outcomes?

Consulting Services

Another approach to supporting faculty with backward design is to provide individual and small group consulting. The Teaching and Learning Center can be an incredibly useful resource, providing initial and ongoing support via individual or small group meetings. If expertise does not exist on campus, or the staff of the Teaching and Learning Center is not able to provide this service due to capacity restraints, colleges might investigate hiring an exter-nal consultant who has expertise in backward design.

This consulting approach is more individualized and not as structured as the faculty learning community approach. Faculty will likely appreciate hav-ing a course design expert as a resource. Consulting services can provide valuable support to faculty as they engage in an incredibly complex task.

MEASURING AND CELEBRATING SUCCESS

Given the impact of backward design on student success, it is critical that colleges encourage faculty to engage in backward design, support faculty in this process, and recognize and celebrate faculty efforts in this area. Colleges can draw attention to the positive impact of course design by sharing assess-ment results and highlighting faculty efforts related to engaging in backward design. Showcasing positive teaching and learning efforts can validate and honor faculty who have engaged in the course design process and encourage others to engage in this work. Positive energy surrounding improved student learning can be contagious.

Assessing teaching and learning practices can be challenging because many factors contribute to student success. However, institutional research and assessment experts on campus can be utilized to help faculty develop an assessment plan. One simple approach is to compare student achievement data of faculty prior to engaging in the course design process to student achievement data of faculty after engaging in the course design process.

In addition to quantitative data such as academic performance and retention, it can also be helpful to gather qualitative data to better understand how a redesigned course impacts student engagement. Qualitative data provides rich information that can help colleges understand the why and how behind quantitative data. For example, student focus groups on their experiences can prove to be helpful when trying to understand how course design impacts student success.

Documenting successful interventions is essential. When faculty work hard to improve student learning, it can be extremely rewarding to see the results of these efforts. In fact, success data can do wonders to the culture on campus. Faculty and staff want to see that their work is making a difference, and this is best illustrated through improved student achievement data.

Disaggregating the data to determine the impact on different populations within the broader campus communities is also important. Overall success rates are often the marker many turn to and this type of data is important. However, colleges committed to equity will also want to know how interventions are impacting different groups of students. Thus, success data by race, gender, and other factors is needed.

Hopefully, the data will show that efforts are making a difference in reducing academic achievement gaps among different student populations, especially those who are typically underserved and underperforming. If not, it is important for faculty to know this so they can explore other options to better support students. The point of assessment, after all, is improvement.

CONCLUDING REMARKS

When courses are developed using the backward design process, student success is more likely. Backward design involves three steps: determining learning outcomes, identifying assessments that will provide evidence that students successfully completed the learning outcomes, and determining which teaching approaches will best support the learning goals and activities. Colleges need to provide support to faculty as they engage in this time-consuming, yet incredibly powerful process of designing or redesigning courses using the backward design framework.

Support can come in many forms. Professional development focused on introducing faculty to the backward design process is a notable first step.

However, faculty will likely need additional support to fully engage in this process. Faculty learning communities and consulting are examples of how colleges can provide ongoing support. Colleges committed to supporting faculty with designing and redesigning courses will undoubtedly move the needle on student success outcomes.

Chapter Four

Evidence-based Teaching and Learning Practices

At the end of this chapter, you will be able to:

1. Explain the importance of faculty using evidence-based teaching and learning practices.
2. Discuss how colleges can support faculty with developing effective syllabi, engaging students, improving lecturing and group work, and teaching online.

Faculty are hired for their expertise in a specific discipline. Although there has been an increased focus on teaching in graduate programs in recent years, most graduate programs do not heavily emphasize pedagogical and andragogical expertise. As a result, faculty do not receive much, if any, formal training in how to be an effective teacher yet teaching is their primary responsibility at many colleges, especially community colleges.

Faculty typically learn to teach through trial and error. Most faculty received very little direction, guidance, or support when they first started teaching. An all-too-common scenario is for a new faculty member, especially a part-time faculty member, to be given a sample syllabus and a textbook and then be sent into the classroom. The new faculty member is then left to figure out how to design and teach the course.

Full and part-time faculty who have been teaching for many years have likely developed their teaching skill set over time, and numerous faculty have become incredibly talented teachers. However, this trial-and-error approach to developing teaching expertise takes time. The lack of training and guidance for new faculty means that students who are in classes with inexperienced teachers will likely be at a disadvantage over others who are taking classes with more experienced faculty members.

As colleges increasingly rely on part-time faculty, the number of inexperienced faculty continues to grow. Almost 50% of the faculty at bachelor degree granting institutions are part-time positions, and this number climbs to more than 65% at community colleges (American Association of University Professors, 2018). According to a national survey, 37% of part-time faculty have only been teaching four years or less (Center for Community College Student Engagement, 2014).

Thus, hundreds of thousands of community college students are being taught by part-time faculty who have very little teaching experience. Unfortunately, research shows that student success outcomes for students taking courses with part-time faculty are lower than the success outcomes for students taking classes with full-time faculty (Ran & Xu, 2017; Yu, Campbell, & Mendoza, 2015). This is clearly problematic.

The lack of professional development and support is likely a key factor in the different student outcomes for part-time versus full-time faculty. Banachowski (1997) cites research showing that part-time faculty who participate in faculty development use methods of teaching that are similar to the ones used by their full-time faculty colleagues. Providing professional development to all faculty is therefore critically important if colleges want to ensure that all students are getting a high-quality learning experience.

Although teaching skills and expertise play a major role in student success, supporting the development of teaching expertise has received very little national attention as colleges engage in guided pathways. Fortunately, national leaders such as Stout (2018), the president of Achieving the Dream, are expressing the urgent need for institutions to put teaching and learning at the core of student success reform efforts. Colleges committed to student success need to devote significant resources to assist faculty with developing and enhancing their teaching skills.

Colleges have an obligation to provide faculty with professional development that will equip them with the knowledge and skills they need to be expert teachers. Colleges that direct resources toward faculty development are positioning themselves well to move the needle on student success outcomes. According to the League for Innovation in the Community College (2018), "Developing instructional resources to the fullest potential is a wise investment in the organization" (p. 7). The importance of institutional support for high-quality teaching cannot be overstated.

Although it is not feasible to provide a comprehensive overview of the body of literature on effective pedagogical and andragogical practices in one chapter, this chapter highlights how colleges can support several evidence-based teaching practices. Specifically, colleges can provide resources and professional development that assist faculty with developing effective syllabi, engaging students at the start of the semester, developing and delivering dynamic lectures, facilitating effective group work, and using effective online teaching strategies.

Assisting faculty in these areas is an excellent way for institutions to improve the student learning experience and ultimately improve student outcomes. Faculty will likely be interested in learning about these effective pedagogical and andragogical approaches because they want to support students. Because each faculty member teaches numerous courses each semester, the impact of instructional change can be quite significant.

DEVELOPING EFFECTIVE SYLLABI

The syllabus is perhaps one of the most underutilized resources in higher education. Unfortunately, the syllabus is often viewed as a document that primarily conveys policies and assignments. Colleges can help faculty realize the value of this document and how it can be used to support student learning.

A well-designed syllabus can serve as a road map for students. Palmer (2017) notes that the syllabus can draw attention to the course learning outcomes so students can see the purpose and relevance of the course. The syllabus can also provide students with information about course expectations and the types of learning tasks that they will need to engage in order to achieve the course learning goals. When students see the connection between learning tasks and the course goals, motivation is likely to be higher.

Colleges can encourage faculty to use this important document to get students excited about the course and their field of study and to begin to foster a connection between the professor and student. Faculty can include welcoming statements that communicate their passion for the field and teaching. Using the syllabus, faculty can also articulate why this course will help students build skills and gain knowledge that will serve them well in their career.

The type of information that is included and the way in which this information is communicated matters. Research has shown that when faculty use a positive tone in their syllabus, students have a more positive view of the course and instructor (Harnish & Bridges, 2011). Faculty can make minor language adjustments to personalize the syllabus, such as using "you" and "I" language instead of "student" and "professor" language. This personalized approach can help foster a positive professor-student connection right at the start of the semester.

To ensure faculty include all the essential information in their syllabus, colleges can provide faculty with exemplary syllabi, a syllabus checklist resource, and a syllabus template. The Teaching and Learning Center can take the lead on finding high-quality sample syllabi and developing resources and templates for faculty.

The checklist can remind faculty about all the various topics such as information about the course, professor, and policies that need to be included. In addition, the checklist can remind faculty about other important elements to consider such as tone and clarity. See Textbox 4.1 for a sample syllabus checklist. Templates can offer standardized language for institutional policies.

TEXTBOX 4.1: THE SYLLABUS CHECKLIST

Reproduced with permission from Stylus Publishing.

Harrington, C., & Thomas, M. (2018). *Designing a motivational syllabus: Creating a learning path for student engagement.* Stylus Publishing.

Syllabus Checklist

Essential Elements

Tone

- What is the tone of the syllabus?
- Is it personal and engaging?
- What emotional reaction do you have to this document?
- Do you have a sense of excitement about the course?

Value and Purpose

- Do you see the value of the course and understand its purpose?
- Are the learning outcomes clearly defined?
- How would you describe this course to someone?

Organization and Clarity

- Do you know what to do to meet with success and how to access help if needed?
- Is it well organized and easy to follow?
- Can you easily see what is expected of you?
- Were enough details provided?
- Does the syllabus provide you with a clear path to success?

- Were visual tools such as charts used to organize the information and clearly communicate information?

Perception of Professor

- How would you describe the professor based on this syllabus?
- Do you expect to be challenged and supported by the professor?
- Do you think the professor is excited to teach this course?
- Do you think the professor believes in you?
- Would you be likely to take courses offered by this professor?

Perception of the Course

- Would you be likely to register for this course?
- What did you like the most about the syllabus?
- What suggestions do you have to make the syllabus better?

Essential Components

Course Information

- Course name and number
- Course description
- Purpose and value of the course
- Course learning outcomes and connection to program learning outcomes
- Learning objectives for modules, units, or classes
- Overview of course content, including topics
- Location, times, days
- Textbooks and supplemental readings
- Calendar of activities

Instructor and Campus Support Information

- Professor name
- Office location and hours
- Contact information: phone, e-mail address
- Welcome statement and teaching philosophy
- Information on available campus resources
- Tips for success

Assignments and Grading Information

- Grading policy, grading scale including weighting of assignments toward final grade
- Assignments and descriptions
- Rationale for assignments and link back to course learning outcomes
- Grading details and rubrics
- Course outline with due dates

Policy Information

- Late and missed work policy
- Attendance policy
- Academic conduct policy, including academic integrity policy
- Disability policy

In addition to providing information about the course, syllabi can also be used to share relevant resources and supports with students. Perrine, Lisle, and Tucker (1995) conducted an interesting study on this topic. Findings from this study showed that students who received a syllabus with six additional words, *please come and talk to me*, indicated they would be more likely to reach out for assistance as compared to students who received the same syllabus without those words.

This provides evidence that the syllabus can be used as a tool to encourage students to reach out for support. Faculty can be required or encouraged to provide their office hours and contact information on their syllabus. Because students may not be familiar with higher education language, it may be important for faculty to share that office hours are specific times for students to meet with faculty. Adding encouraging language such as "please come and talk to me" is recommended. Faculty can also be encouraged to provide information about on-campus resources that students may find beneficial.

Some colleges create a syllabus template that can be shared with faculty. This can be particularly helpful to new faculty who probably do not have much experience with developing syllabi. Syllabus templates can provide a way to consistently share policy information with students.

It is important that policies are developed with student success in mind. Bombardieri (2019) reported on how a policy change allowing students to submit work late at Pasadena City College is having a positive impact on student success, especially for Latino students. Unfortunately, many syllabi contain policies that can be characterized as rigid and punitive in nature. Conversations about the impact that institutional and classroom policies can have on student success need to take place.

If a college decides to use a standardized syllabus, it will want to avoid being overly prescriptive to allow faculty some freedom to personalize the syllabus. Students will likely respond more positively to a syllabus that lets them get to know their faculty members and see their unique approach to the course. Thus, a balance between consistency and personalization must be achieved.

As faculty engage in the syllabus redesign process, colleges will want to find ways to showcase revised syllabi. Faculty can be invited to share their before and after syllabi at campus meetings. Colleges may also want to showcase exemplary syllabi on their website.

To determine which syllabi to showcase, a peer review process can be implemented. After participating in syllabus training, faculty can be invited to serve as peer reviewers of syllabi. Reviewers can use a syllabus rubric such as the one published by Harrington and Thomas (2018) to determine whether to showcase the syllabus on the website. Faculty who create syllabi that were selected as exemplars could document this in their tenure and promotion packets.

ENGAGING STUDENTS AT THE START OF THE SEMESTER

"Research shows that the more actively engaged students are—with college faculty and staff, with other students, and with the subject matter they study—the more likely they are to learn, to stick with their studies, and to attain their academic goals" (Community College Survey of Student Engagement, 2007, p. 4). Although student engagement can begin prior to a student attending class, the classroom is where student engagement happens in significant ways, especially at community colleges or colleges with high numbers of commuter students. The first day of class can be especially important in fostering student engagement and connection.

Through professional development, colleges can help faculty see the important role the first day of class plays in terms of student engagement. More specifically, colleges can help faculty discover how the first day of class can be used to promote a sense of belonging, get students excited about the course, and begin the process of building student knowledge and skills in the course material (Lang, n.d.). Helping students connect to one another, their professor, and the course content on day one will increase student engagement and learning.

Before colleges focus on assisting faculty with reimagining their first day of class, it may be important to engage in some case-making. Case-making involves sharing the rationale for why faculty would want to approach the first day of class differently in addition to providing supporting evidence for the proposed changes. Faculty, especially those teaching courses with significant content demands, may not see the value of using time during the first day of class for icebreakers or other activities designed to foster connections and engagement.

There is a significant body of literature that highlights the importance of the first day of class (Baker, 2012; McGinley & Jones, 2014; Vander Schee, 2007), but faculty may not be aware of this research. Colleges can share the research on the impact of the first day of class in workshops or other outlets such as teaching newsletters. Sharing research studies, such as the study by Foster and Hermann (2011) that shows the long-lasting impact of using a reciprocal interview on the first day of class activity, can persuade faculty to reconsider how they approach the first day of class.

In addition to encouraging faculty to use icebreakers to help students feel comfortable in the learning environment and get to know one another, colleges can also provide faculty with suggested icebreaker activities. Harrington and Thomas (2018) suggest using icebreakers that directly relate to the course content. One example of an icebreaker that can be used in all disciplines is the Jigsaw Classroom syllabus review. The Jigsaw Classroom approach has been shown to positively impact learning (Walker & Crogan, 1998).

The Jigsaw Classroom syllabus review activity requires students to work in structured groups while exploring the content and structure of the course through reviewing the syllabus. This activity involves the following steps:

1. Assign students to small groups of approximately four students. This is called the home base group.
2. Each member of the home base group needs to select a different section of the syllabus (e.g., learning outcomes, policies, assignments, grading information, course schedule).
3. New groups are then formed. All students working on the same section work together in what is called an expert group. They are tasked with reviewing their assigned section of the syllabus and identifying the key points from this section that they will bring back to share with their home base group. During this part of the activity, faculty will need to ensure that groups are identifying the most important points.
4. Students then return to their home base group and each member takes a few minutes to share the most important points from their assigned section.
5. A brief large group discussion can take place where unanswered questions can be addressed by the faculty member.

This approach is particularly useful if the instructor is planning to use Jigsaw Classroom activities throughout the semester. Using an activity on the first day of class that is reflective of how the class will be taught not only engages students but also prepares them for future learning tasks (Gannon, 2016).

It is important to communicate to faculty that icebreakers are not the only way to engage students. Robinson (2019), for example, investigated the value of a first day of class activity where students had to write questions about the field of psychology and then discuss their thoughts and responses with classmates prior to the lecture. Results revealed that students who participated in this activity, as compared to those who did not participate in this activity, had higher levels of engagement and a more favorable impression of the class.

Thus, faculty can also be encouraged to use a variety of first day of class activities. Icebreakers, especially those that are discipline specific, can help students develop a sense of community in the classroom. Activities that are designed to get students engaged with the discipline content from day one are also valuable.

Providing full and part-time faculty with models of effective first day of class lessons can be helpful. Teaching and Learning Centers can assist by identifying several examples of icebreakers that would work well in many different disciplines as well as icebreakers that are discipline specific. There are many examples that can be drawn from the literature and professional organizations. For example, Eggleston and Smith (2004) share several icebreaker activities that work well in psychology classes.

In addition to sample activities from the literature, faculty can also be encouraged to share examples they have used in their classrooms. Sharing different approaches to the first day with colleagues is a good use of time at faculty meetings. Giving faculty the time and space to have meaningful conversations about how to make the most of the first day of class sends a message about the importance of engaging students from day one.

If faculty have not already done so, colleges can encourage them to assess first day of class activities. Gathering and analyzing data on how the first day of class activities impact student success can help faculty see the important role they play in student success. Colleges can also share institutional-level data from surveys such as the Community College Survey of Student Engagement (CCSSE) to help faculty see the connection between initial student experiences in the classroom and student engagement and success.

Faculty find it very rewarding to see how their efforts are making a difference. This can increase faculty motivation to continue their efforts at improving teaching practices. It is therefore important for colleges to find ways to document and share success.

Another way to bring attention to the importance of the first day is through the student voice. Colleges can ask students to share testimonials about how the first day of class experiences were beneficial to them. These testimonials and examples can be featured in the student newspaper or on social media. Faculty enjoy hearing how their actions impact their students. Student stories can inspire and motivate faculty to reimagine their first day of class with student engagement in mind.

LECTURING FOR LEARNING

The lecture is still the most widely used teaching strategy. There is research evidence that shows lecturing can be effective, especially with novice student learners (Baeten, Dochy, & Struyven, 2013; Clark, Kirschner, & Sweller, 2012). Thus, it makes sense for lectures to be used more frequently in introductory-level courses.

As with all teaching techniques, the lecture can be done well or poorly. Unfortunately, poorly executed lectures often result in many believing the lecture is an ineffective teaching method. This is not the case if the lecture is performed well.

When colleges suggest that faculty use active learning strategies instead of lecturing, faculty can get frustrated that the teaching method they have relied on throughout the years is not being validated. Harrington and Zakrajsek (2017) suggest that active learning can take place during a dynamic, interactive lecture. In other words, it doesn't have to be an either-or scenario. Helping faculty use evidence-based practices when they lecture will likely result in improved student learning.

There are several ways colleges can support faculty with using the lecturing teaching method effectively. A professional development program focused on incorporating active learning components into the lecture is one of the most commonly used approaches. Colleges can also use the classroom observation process as an opportunity to support faculty with improving their lectures. In addition, colleges can modify self-evaluation processes to include redesigned lectures.

Focusing on lecturing in professional development programming is beneficial for several reasons. Because the lecture is still the most frequently used teaching method, offering workshops on this topic can be validating to faculty. Often, faculty may interpret professional development programs as a message that they are not using effective methods and they need to significantly revamp their teaching style. This can be discouraging or overwhelming. Faculty will likely perceive professional development on lecturing as validating. Because this type of professional development is building on a familiar skill set, it is more likely that faculty will implement the techniques learned. In fact, several of the strategies that colleges can share with faculty can be immediately applied to their teaching practices.

Professional development programs can focus on several evidence-based practices that will increase student learning during lectures. For example, helping faculty determine and clearly communicate the primary learning objectives or big ideas for each lecture can help structure and organize the lesson, bringing emphasis to the most salient points. In addition, assisting faculty with identifying active learning breaks that can be incorporated into the lecture can help students digest and process the information being learned.

As experts in the field, faculty can easily identify the key learning objectives, major themes, or big ideas for each lecture. However, students often struggle to differentiate the important from the less important so they may not be able to easily identify the big ideas of each lecture (Hrepic, Zollman, & Rebello, 2004). Clearly communicating and drawing attention to the most important concepts can be incredibly helpful to students. Knowing the big ideas enables students to more easily take in details related to the subject matter.

Faculty can be encouraged to share the three most important concepts from each lecture with students prior to the lecture and then to emphasize these major concepts during the lecture. This can be accomplished by faculty simply stating they are introducing the first important concept or through other techniques such as a gesture or a dramatic pause. At the end of each lecture, faculty can then summarize the three main points from the lecture.

One of the biggest mistakes faculty make when lecturing is neglecting to build in opportunities for students to reflect on what was just learned and engage with the material in some way. Thus, colleges need to help faculty see the value of incorporating active learning breaks into the lecture and strategies for doing so. There is a significant amount of research illustrating the value of this approach.

For example, research shows that student learning significantly increases when students are given three two-minute pauses during a lecture to share and compare notes or are given opportunities to write summaries of what they just learned (Davis & Hult, 1997; Ruhl, Hughes, & Schloss, 1987). Giving students time in class to review and revise their notes with a partner was found to be more beneficial than having students independently revise their notes outside of class (Luo, Kiewrar, & Samuelson, 2016). Sharing this research with faculty will illuminate the need to incorporate strategies such as these into their lectures.

In addition to using active learning techniques at the start of class, faculty can also be encouraged to use active learning breaks throughout the lecture. A good strategy that can be recommended to faculty is for them to use a different active learning break after each big idea (Harrington & Zakrajsek, 2017). This way, students will have an opportunity to reflect on and cognitively engage with each of the three major concepts for each lecture.

There are a variety of active learning breaks that can be used. Some powerful ones include the "Turn and Talk" where students discuss the concept for a few minutes, the one-minute paper where students write a summary of what they learned, and a quick quiz using an online polling tool where teams are allowed to discuss their responses to questions about the content just learned. Using active learning breaks is a powerful way for faculty to enhance student learning during the lecture.

Ending the lecture with an active learning exercise that gives students an opportunity to summarize all three big ideas is also advisable. Too often faculty use the last few minutes of class to cram in more content. This doesn't usually result in increased student learning. Faculty who use the last few minutes of class for students to engage in reflection and retrieval related to content just learned will likely find that student learning increases.

In addition to providing support through professional development, colleges can support faculty by focusing on the lecture in classroom observations and through the use of self-evaluation tools. During classroom observation processes, for example, administrators or colleagues conducting the observation can provide feedback on how clearly the big ideas were communicated and provide suggestions about how and when to incorporate active learning breaks into the lecture.

Similarly, when faculty engage in the self-evaluation process, colleges can require faculty to reflect on and write about how they organize a lecture. Faculty can also be asked to describe how they incorporate active learning breaks into their lectures. Reflective activities such as this one can result in improved teaching practices.

FACILITATING COLLABORATION AND TEAMWORK SKILLS VIA GROUP WORK

Employers are looking for employees who have strong soft or transferable skills. Communication and collaboration are among the top skills employers are seeking (Koc, 2011; Robles, 2012). Consequently, course learning outcomes will often reference the development of these soft skills. Helping faculty select teaching methods that align to course learning outcomes and then supporting them in using these teaching methods effectively paves the way for student learning. One of the best ways to help students develop communication and collaboration skills is through group projects.

Unfortunately, group work is often dreaded by faculty and students alike. Students often dislike group work because of prior experiences that were negative in nature. For example, students often complain that one group member had to do all the work while others did not pull their weight and contribute in a meaningful way. Faculty find group work frustrating because they often need to spend a significant amount of time mediating conflict in groups and they also find it challenging to grade group work fairly.

Too often, the higher-performing students earn lower grades because of their lower-performing group members, and lower-performing students can have their grades inflated because of the work of their higher-performing group members (Almond, 2009). Due to these challenges, some faculty opt not to do group work. This is problematic because students are then missing out on the opportunity to develop essential skills needed in the world of work.

Providing faculty with professional development on how to effectively engage students in group work is important. It can increase the likelihood they will incorporate group work into their teaching practices and that students learn these essential skills. Faculty can be encouraged to structure group work in a way where there is accountability and interdependence (Millis, 2002).

Accountability refers to a structure and process that ensures all members contribute to the group project in meaningful ways. Interdependence refers to a group activity that will only be successful if group members work collaboratively with other members. In other words, group projects need to require teamwork and cooperation.

Professional development programs can focus on how to structure group projects in a way that is likely to have positive outcomes. Too often, students are asked to engage in group work with little to no support in how to effectively function in a group. Faculty can, therefore, be provided with guidance and support on how to best prepare students for group work. Research has shown that students who are trained on how to be a productive group member and work collaboratively with their peers are more likely to have higher levels of learning (Prichard, Stratford, & Bizo, 2006).

Faculty can be encouraged to use class time to train and support students with group work. This way, the faculty member is available to monitor progress and provide support as needed throughout the process. It is much easier to ensure all members are participating and making significant and meaningful contributions to the group when groups are working on projects during class.

When students are working with group members during class, faculty members can be encouraged to check in with groups about their progress. Faculty should be cautioned about asking generic questions such as "How is it going?" This will not likely be beneficial because students will typically reply with generic answers such as "good."

Instead, faculty can ask groups targeted questions about what they have accomplished thus far. After hearing student responses about progress, the faculty member can provide guidance and support as needed. This immediate, verbal feedback can be extremely valuable to students. Groups can either move forward with confidence that they are on the right track or benefit from specific suggestions about the task to get back on track.

Faculty will also benefit from professional development programming that specifically focuses on grading group projects. Colleges can provide faculty with research on this topic and then encourage them to have conversations with colleagues about the pros and cons of different approaches to grading group work. For example, faculty may not be aware that giving all the students in a group the same grade, often referred to as the group grade, can have negative consequences. King and Behnke (2005), for example, note that group grades can have a negative impact on interpersonal relationships in the class.

Another primary challenge with the group grade is that it does not often tell an accurate story about an individual student's performance (Almond, 2009). Based on this information, faculty may need support with determining alternative methods to the group grade. For example, faculty may want to rely more heavily on individual assignments that are incorporated into a group project.

To promote accountability and ensure that all students are making significant contributions, colleges can encourage faculty to require students to first complete an individual assignment prior to having students interact with group members. Sarfo and Ellen (2011) report that individual assignments prior to group work, along with providing students with a strong foundational base of related knowledge, results in positive outcomes. Every member needs to contribute when this approach is used.

This approach ensures that all group members are bringing something to the table at the initial group meeting. It also allows faculty to evaluate the quality of each individual's contribution. Building in formative, individual assessments can set the stage for success by ensuring students have the adequate training and preparation prior to engaging in a group project.

In addition to providing workshops and training on how to effectively teach using groups, colleges will also want to find ways to provide ongoing support to faculty. As mentioned previously, group work can be challenging. Having consultants available through the Teaching and Learning Center and ongoing faculty learning communities on effective group work will provide faculty with the support they need to successfully address challenges encountered.

TEACHING ONLINE

Interestingly, colleges often provide higher levels of support to faculty teaching in online environments as compared to faculty teaching in-person classes, even though most classes are still being taught in a face-to-face format. Colleges often have an instructional design team that provides numerous professional development workshops to faculty on how to design an online course. It is also common for colleges to require faculty to participate in training prior to being assigned an online class to teach. These supports and structures can be very helpful to faculty.

Although colleges may have more resources devoted to assisting faculty with teaching online, much of the training provided is exclusively focused on how to use technology tools rather than assisting faculty with course design and teaching methods. As technology is ever-changing, faculty will appreciate how-to sessions where they can develop new technology skills. Learning different course management systems can be particularly challenging for part-time faculty who may be teaching at different colleges where different learning management systems are used.

Training needs to go beyond how-to sessions. Improving student success outcomes will require faculty to consider how to best use technology to promote learning. Colleges will need to evaluate the type of current support being provided to ensure that high levels of support in both designing and teaching effectively in an online environment are provided. Although this support is typically designed for faculty teaching online courses, all faculty can benefit from professional development related to online learning as most courses today have online components.

Perhaps one of the greatest challenges associated with online learning is developing a sense of community and connection virtually. To assist faculty with designing an online learning community, colleges can share models and frameworks with faculty. For example, Garrison, Anderson, and Archer's (2000) community of inquiry framework emphasizes the importance of social presence, cognitive presence, and teaching presence in the online environment.

In poorly designed online classes, students can quickly feel isolated and disconnected. It is therefore critical for faculty to build a learning community within the virtual classroom to help students feel connected to them as the instructor, their classmates, and the content. There are numerous strategies that faculty can employ to build these connections.

In addition to providing frameworks to faculty, colleges can provide examples of how to build this sense of community of learners in the online environment. Some simple strategies to build connection include starting the semester with a getting-to-know-you discussion that includes video introductions. Research has shown that icebreakers in online classes are valuable, increasing a student's sense of social presence in the class (Dixon, Crooks, & Henry, 2006).

Faculty can also incorporate learning activities that require students to work with partners or small groups. Online synchronous and asynchronous tools can be used to help students connect with group members, share resources, and cocreate academic products. Banna, Grace Lin, Stewart, and Fialkowski (2015) found that students who participated in synchronous learning reported these activities were valuable and increased their engagement; however, they caution that synchronous learning may contribute to inequality because not all students were able to attend the live sessions.

To help students feel connected to the professor, the professor can create video mini-lectures or announcements. Students are more likely to feel connected to faculty who are regularly in the virtual classroom. This can be seen through contributions in discussions and also through the regular, personalized feedback provided.

One of the primary tools that have been used to create a sense of community in online courses is the discussion board. Online discussions can help students connect with one another and deeply explore the course content. However, it can be challenging for faculty to identify question prompts and follow-up questions that foster meaningful conversations. Faculty are also unsure of how involved they should be in discussions. Because online discussions are very different from discussions that take place in the classroom, colleges will want to provide faculty with resources and professional development on best practices in online discussion boards.

Aloni and Harrington (2018) encourage faculty to provide clear expectations for initial and follow-up contributions to the conversation such as whether students need to reference outside sources. They also emphasize the importance of creating question prompts that facilitate critical thinking skills and provide opportunities for multiple perspectives and ideas to be shared. Unfortunately, many online discussions begin with a general question prompt with directions for students to interact with at least two classmates without the purpose or goal of these interactions being shared.

An approach that will likely lead to higher quality conversations is asking students to interact with classmates by asking and answering Socratic questions about the initial posts (Aloni & Harrington, 2018). Faculty can provide students with sample Socratic questions that they can refer to when interacting with classmates. Faculty can also model this approach through their contributions to the conversation.

Colleges can also share research about the role of the faculty in managing and contributing to online conversations. Research shows that students contribute the most to online conversations when faculty are participating at a moderate level (Morris, Xu, & Finnegan, 2005). Faculty presence and involvement in conversations are important.

Thompson (2006) points out that if faculty participate too much, it can stifle the conversation, and if faculty participate too little, students will not view the activity as important. Too much or too little faculty involvement results in fewer student contributions and learning. Thus, faculty will need to work on finding the right balance.

Although the discussion is one of the primary methods used in online teaching, it is important for faculty to recognize that online learning platforms offer many ways to help students engage with one another and the course content. Not every learning outcome will be best achieved by discussion. As previously emphasized, teaching methods need to be selected as part of the backward design process.

Thus, relying primarily or exclusively on online discussions each week to facilitate learning will probably not lead to the desired outcomes. Just as in traditional classrooms, a variety of teaching methods will be needed. Faculty can be encouraged to use a combination of lectures, small and large group activities, and discussions depending on the learning goal for each lesson.

Lecturing online is very different from lecturing in a face-to-face environment. Most notably, online lectures are usually much shorter in duration. Longer lectures are typically divided into smaller segments. Faculty will likely appreciate having support as they develop and create online lectures. For example, faculty can be provided training on how to use technology tools such as screencast and video and the value of incorporating online lectures into their classes.

In addition to becoming familiar with the technology tools, faculty also need to consider how to best engage students via online lectures. Faculty can be encouraged to develop effective PowerPoint slides using Mayer's (2009) multimedia principles and to share real-world examples of concepts. Providing support to faculty can result in increased confidence in using technology tools effectively. Faculty who are more confident in their ability to use technology will be more inclined to incorporate technology into their teaching.

To meet the needs of both full and part-time faculty, it may be best to provide these training sessions and support in a variety of ways. In addition to providing in-person support via individual meetings or workshops, posting tutorials online is advisable. Faculty are often working on course development late in the evening or on the weekends when on-campus support may not be possible. Online options will provide faculty with the resources they need when they need them. This can be particularly helpful to part-time faculty whose full-time employment makes it impossible for them to take advantage of on-campus training scheduled during the day.

Colleges may want to consider partnering with other institutions to provide support services related to online instruction. This can be a great way to maximize the limited resources available on each campus. Partnerships can enable colleges to take advantage of consortium-type pricing for external support to ensure that faculty have what they need when they need it in order to develop and deliver effective online courses as well as in-person courses with strong online components.

CONCLUDING REMARKS

Supporting faculty by providing professional development opportunities that emphasize evidence-based teaching practices is one of the best ways colleges can move the needle in terms of improving student success outcomes. Faculty have typically been hired for their discipline expertise but may have had little to no training on how to teach effectively. Colleges committed to student success reform efforts such as guided pathways need to make teaching and learning a priority. Investing in a Teaching and Learning Center that can develop and implement professional development opportunities is an excellent strategy.

At professional development programs, faculty can learn about the scholarship of teaching and learning and how to apply the research in their classroom. Colleges can help faculty see the value of the syllabus and first day of class activities. Faculty will also benefit from learning about the research on how to maximize learning through lectures, group work, and online teaching methods. Research shows that student learning improves when faculty use evidence-based approaches in their classroom, both online and in person.

Chapter Five

Assessing Instructor Effectiveness

At the end of this chapter, you will be able to:

1. Describe how using an improvement lens for assessing instructor effectiveness can improve student outcomes.
2. Evaluate current practices related to assessing instructor effectiveness.
3. Develop or revise processes and practices related to assessing instructor effectiveness to focus on improving teaching and learning.

In addition to providing faculty with high-quality professional development and ongoing support related to effectively designing and delivering courses, colleges committed to improving student success outcomes will also want to assess instructor effectiveness. Colleges need to determine if professional development and support are translating into effective teaching practices in the classroom. Ensuring learning, an essential practice within the guided pathways framework, is best accomplished when faculty create welcoming learning environments and provide highly effective instruction.

Instructor effectiveness is often assessed to make personnel decisions such as whether to reappoint, promote, or tenure a faculty member. However, colleges engaged in guided pathways reform efforts will want to consider how to enhance the process of assessing instructor effectiveness on their campus so that teaching and learning practices are improved. Like assessment practices that take place across the institution, assessing instructor effectiveness can be approached with the goal of improvement in mind.

More specifically, colleges will want to determine which evidence-based teaching practices and skills are being used effectively by faculty and which skills need to be further developed. Drew and Klopper (2014) recommend analyzing data from multiple sources in order to determine target areas for professional development. A comprehensive review of data on instructor effectiveness will guide colleges as they determine how to best support faculty with implementing evidence-based practices in their classrooms so that students learn and achieve more.

Colleges already use a variety of methods to assess instructor effectiveness. For example, student evaluations, classroom observations, and self-assessments are commonly used methods. However, colleges will want to review and reevaluate the current assessment methods and processes to determine if they are providing faculty with specific and meaningful feedback that leads to improved teaching practices.

Unfortunately, less than one-third of faculty surveyed indicated that the scholarship of teaching and learning was included as criteria in evaluations (Gurung, Ansburg, Alexander, Lawrence, & Johnson, 2008). Current methods may not be emphasizing evidence-based teaching practices. It is therefore likely that colleges will need to modify current processes and practices in order to shift the focus to improving teaching and learning.

STUDENT EVALUATIONS AND FEEDBACK

Students are clearly not experts on how to teach, but their experiences and perspectives can provide important data for faculty. Faculty can seek student feedback at multiple points in the semester using a variety of formal and informal methods. The two most commonly used approaches to gathering student feedback are the student evaluation and the mid-semester focus group.

Student Evaluations

Student evaluations are one of the most widely used tools to assess instructor effectiveness, but there are many challenges and biases with this tool. Colleges are cautioned not to rely too heavily on student evaluations to assess instructor effectiveness. Stark and Freishtat (2014) found that student evaluations do not accurately measure teaching effectiveness and noted that student evaluations "seem to be influenced by the gender, ethnicity, and attractiveness of the instructor" (p. 19).

Students are not positioned to be evaluators of teaching effectiveness and are not skilled at doing so. Thus, the data obtained from student evaluations needs to be interpreted carefully and only in the context of other data sources. The American Sociological Association (2019) recommends that student evaluations "should be part of a holistic assessment that includes peer observations, reviews of teaching materials, and instructor self-reflections" (p. 2).

Colleges using student evaluations will want to have conversations about what type of valuable information can be gathered from the student perspective. Student evaluations are a window into how students perceive the learning experience. Thus, questions about student experiences in the classroom and their reactions to these experiences may be of value. A few examples that tap into the student experience are as follows:

- I felt (welcomed, respected, included) in the class.
- The syllabus provided me with information about (what I would learn and what was expected of me).
- The instructor used teaching techniques that kept me engaged.
- The feedback I was provided by the instructor was (helpful and encouraging).
- I gained (confidence, knowledge, and skills) in this class.

Stark and Freishtat (2014) suggest that colleges avoid asking students about the overall effectiveness of an instructor as they do not have the expertise to answer this question, and this type of question is significantly influenced by factors that are not relevant to instructor effectiveness. Thus, a question such as, "Did the instructor use effective teaching methods?" would not be appropriate.

If the purpose of assessing instructor effectiveness is to improve teaching practices, colleges will need to look beyond student evaluations. Research has shown that simply providing faculty with access to student evaluations does not lead to improved teaching. In a study that analyzed student evaluations for a diverse group of almost 200 instructors over thirteen years, it was found that teacher effectiveness was relatively stable over time, suggesting that the student evaluation feedback that they regularly received did not result in instructors changing their teaching strategies (Marsh, 2007).

However, research does show that if instructors are provided with consultation services and engage in developing an action plan for improvement after being shown student evaluation feedback, teaching skills do improve. This was illustrated in an interesting experimental study conducted by Knol, Veld, Vorst, van Driel, and Mellenbergh (2013) that compared instructor effectiveness of instructors who were only provided with student evaluation feedback versus those who received consultation sessions along with student evaluation feedback during the semester. Results indicated that instructors who received consultation services had higher levels of instructor effectiveness as compared to those who did not receive consultation services.

These findings suggest that using tools such as student evaluations in isolation will not lead to improved teaching. Colleges will need to do more than simply provide student evaluation feedback to instructors and hope that instructors will take action to improve their teaching skills. Faculty will need additional support and guidance in order to make significant improvements to their teaching.

Mid-Semester Focus Groups

Faculty may also want to gather student feedback during the semester so that timely modifications can benefit current students. One formal approach to gathering student feedback is the mid-semester focus group. The mid-semester focus group involves asking a colleague, often associated with the Teaching and Learning Center, to come to a class and conduct a 30-minute focus group (Payette & Brown, 2018).

If possible, it is advisable to have two colleagues in attendance so that one can take on the role of facilitator and the other can take on the role of the recorder. During the focus group, students are asked what is helping and hindering their learning and progress in the course and what suggestions, if any, they have for improving the course. It is important to note that the instructor is not present during the focus group and therefore student responses are anonymous.

After students have some time to discuss their responses to the questions in a small group, the facilitator then engages the class in a large group discussion. The recorder documents their responses, including information about whether the thoughts shared are representative of the majority or just a few members of the class. This can be accomplished by asking students to raise their hands or responding via a polling tool if they agree with the comment or suggestion.

At the conclusion of the focus group, the facilitator and recorder will summarize the findings in a user-friendly report that is shared with the faculty member. The focus group facilitator, recorder, and faculty member can opt to meet in order to discuss the comments and suggestions provided by students. At this meeting, an action plan for improvement should be developed.

Out-of-class focus groups or virtual focus groups can be used if faculty do not want to use class time for this purpose. However, student participation will obviously be more challenging and the feedback will therefore not be representative of the entire class. In-class focus groups will provide faculty with the most meaningful information because all students participate, but information from even just a few students in an out-of-class focus group can still be useful.

CLASSROOM OBSERVATIONS

Classroom observations are the only way to directly observe teaching and are therefore an essential part of assessing instructor effectiveness. Most classroom observations take place in a face-to-face format, but with technology, virtual observations can also be used. Research has shown that peer classroom observations significantly and positively correlate with student achievement of learning outcomes and are therefore much more valuable than student evaluations (Galbraith & Merrill, 2012).

Consequently, colleges can have higher levels of confidence in data from classroom observations as compared to student evaluations. Although other assessment methods can be used to provide meaningful feedback to faculty, there really is no substitute for a direct observation of teaching practices. Colleges will therefore want to ensure that classroom observations are one of the methods used to assess instructor effectiveness.

Unfortunately, classroom observations are typically used for evaluative purposes only. Full-time faculty are often observed by colleagues or a chairperson as part of the reappointment, tenure, and promotion processes. Part-time faculty may also have to be observed prior to being reappointed for another term. Davys and Jones (2007) suggest that peer observations be approached through a supportive versus punitive lens. It is important for colleges and faculty to see that the value of classroom observations extend beyond evaluation. Course observations are an essential tool that can be used to facilitate improved teaching and learning.

Classroom Observation Template

Colleges will want to review current forms and processes for classroom observations. Many colleges have used the same system or template for classroom observations for years. Colleges invested in improving teaching and learning processes will find it helpful to take a step back to determine if their current processes and observation forms are accomplishing their goals of improving teaching and learning.

Key stakeholders need to determine what constitutes effective teaching and what type of feedback would be most helpful to faculty. The forms and processes can then be modified to provide helpful feedback aimed at improving student success outcomes. Harrington and Zakrajsek (2017) suggest including the following components in the classroom observation report:

- Syllabus feedback
- Summary of pre-meeting including target areas for feedback
- Lesson format (type of lecture, use of activities)
- Summary of the observed class including time line and sequencing of activities
- Demonstration of content expertise
- Organization and clarity of the lesson
- Effectiveness of engagement strategies
- Meaningful use of technology
- Student engagement and classroom management
- Strength summary of what worked well

- Suggestions for growth and improvement
- Summary of post-observation meeting including an action plan

Classroom Observation Process

Teaching is most likely to improve if the faculty and observer engage in meaningful conversations about teaching and learning prior to and after the observation. Faculty will appreciate being able to converse with a peer who has contextual knowledge from being in the classroom during the observation visit. The classroom observation process, therefore, needs to go beyond a written report and include opportunities for conversation.

Using a three-step process for classroom observations can ensure ample opportunity for discussions about teaching and learning to take place. The three steps in the classroom observation process are:

- the pre-observation meeting
- the classroom observation
- the post-observation meeting

At the pre-meeting, the faculty member can provide the observer with the syllabus and an overview of the course. When the observer has knowledge of the learning activities and tasks that led up to the lesson and the ultimate learning goals, this contextualizes the lesson. At the pre-meeting, faculty can also be asked about which aspect of teaching they would like feedback on. For instance, if the faculty member is using a new teaching technique, they may want specific feedback about how effectively they implemented this technique.

In addition to discussing the course in general, logistics can be addressed at the pre-meeting. For example, the instructor and observer will need to decide on a mutually agreeable date and time for the observation. Other details such as whether the observer will be introduced can also be attended to at the pre-meeting.

During the observation, the observer simply documents the lesson. To maximize time, the observer can use a laptop to record the observations so there is no need to transcribe notes later. The observer can type directly into the template, documenting behavioral observations for the different categories or areas being assessed. Observers should aim to provide specific feedback as this will be most helpful.

Direct observational data can be recorded in several different ways. For instance, the observer can keep a running record of the class activities. Observers can also document communication patterns. Providing faculty with observational data is nonjudgmental and can provide an excellent starting point for meaningful conversations about teaching and learning.

A running record provides faculty with a document that captures the different learning activities used and the amount of class time devoted to each activity. This observational data can be very valuable to the faculty member. For instance, the faculty member may be surprised to discover that a discussion took as long as it did or that they only gave students a few minutes for a complex task that required more time. This direct observational data can help faculty engage in better time management moving forward.

The observer can also document faculty and student behaviors. The observer can provide feedback about instructor actions that can impact learning. For example, the observer might notice that the instructor stands in front of the slides being projected, making it difficult for students to see the visual aid. Because the observer often sits at the back of the room, they can easily see whether students are on or off task when using technology tools such as laptops or mobile devices and share this information with the instructor.

Another type of direct behavioral evidence can come in the form of a communication chart. Malu (2015) describes two types of communication tools that can be used to provide the faculty member with observational data on communication patterns. The first is called a T-chart where the observer simply draws the letter T on a blank piece of paper. Every time the instructor talks, a mark is made on the left side of the T and every time a student talks, a mark is made on the right side of the T. This tool enables faculty to see the instructor-to-student ratio of time spent talking during the lesson.

The second tool described by Malu (2015) is the seating chart tool. To use the seating chart tool, the observer documents communication patterns with lines. In other words, if the instructor asks a student a question, a line would be drawn from the instructor to that student. If students engage in a conversation, lines between the students participating in the conversation would be drawn. This seating chart tool can be used to illustrate who communicated with whom during the lesson.

Receiving this direct data about communication patterns can be an eye-opening experience for the faculty member. The faculty member may be surprised to discover that most of their interactions were with just a few students or that all but a few students engaged in the discussion. Faculty can use this tool to determine if there were differences in their communication patterns with students based on gender, race, or other factors.

In addition to the behavioral observational data, the observer can also provide a summary statement that brings attention to and highlights what went well and provide suggestions to improve teaching and ultimately student learning. This is the part of the observation report that uses the professional expertise of the observer. It is important for faculty to understand that suggestions do not necessarily imply that the faculty was ineffective.

Rather, suggestions can provide alternative approaches to consider and to introduce or share evidence-based teaching strategies that may add value to the learning experience. There are numerous ways that instructors can effectively use evidence-based practices. In addition to providing overall feedback on the lesson, the observer will also need to provide specific feedback on target areas identified during the pre-observation.

Prior to sharing the classroom observation report, faculty can be asked to write a self-assessment of the lesson. Faculty can use the same template the observer uses. The self-assessment can then be compared to the one completed by the outside observer. Faculty typically report that this self-reflective activity is worthwhile and that it adds value to the conversation that takes place during the post-observation meeting.

Often, the observer shares the written classroom observation report with the faculty member prior to the post-observation meeting. This provides the faculty member with an opportunity to review and reflect on the content, comparing the observations from this report with their own assessment of the lesson. An additional advantage of sharing the report ahead of time is that it maximizes the use of the post-observation meeting time. More time will be available for clarifications, questions, and, most importantly, action planning.

Post-observation meetings can begin with a comparison of the self-assessment and observational assessment of the lesson. The focus should be on identifying areas of strength and growth. Together, the faculty member and observer can develop an action plan for improving teaching and learning practices. The action plan will often include using resources and support offered by the Teaching and Learning Center.

To keep action and improvement at the forefront of conversations, the action plan should be used as the starting point for the next observation. During the next pre-meeting, faculty can report their progress on the goals previously identified. In fact, colleges may even want to ask faculty to write a brief progress report prior to the next observation cycle.

In addition to tracking how teaching strategies have changed, colleges will also want to encourage faculty to assess the effectiveness of these changes. In other words, did modifying teaching strategies result in increased learning? Course- and program-level assessment processes can be used for this purpose. As mentioned previously, disaggregating student performance data will enable faculty to see the impact of modifying teaching strategies for different student populations.

Training Observers

Because of the important role of classroom observations in improving teaching and learning, it is essential that colleges invest in training and supporting chairpersons and faculty who will serve as observers. Too often, observers are given this important task without much guidance or training.

The Teaching and Learning Center staff can develop and conduct training on how to conduct classroom observations and provide feedback that will result in improved teaching and learning. If colleges are shifting the focus from evaluation toward improvement, all observers will need to be trained in this framework for the classroom observation process. In addition to participating in training prior to conducting a classroom observation, observers will also benefit from ongoing support, especially when they need to provide more significant guidance to an instructor.

During training sessions, using classroom observations for the purpose of improvement needs to be emphasized. With the improvement goal in mind, administrators and faculty participants can practice documenting behaviors, writing summaries, and providing recommendations. One effective training approach is to show brief videos of faculty teaching and ask participants to write a brief report and role-play how they would give feedback to the instructor.

Facilitators may want to model the process prior to having participants engage in role-play practices. This hands-on approach will likely lead to lively dialogue among participants about how to effectively provide both positive and constructive feedback to instructors. Faculty and chairpersons will increase their confidence in their ability to conduct effective classroom observations with practice.

The training facilitators can provide model observation reports. These examples can be especially helpful to faculty or chairpersons for whom conducting classroom observations is a new task. Participants who have experience conducting observations can also be encouraged to share sample reports with identifying information extracted. The training is an opportunity for colleges to emphasize the supportive role of observers and to share templates and examples of reports that were designed with improving teaching and learning in mind.

Capacity for Classroom Observations

Revising templates and training observers can set the stage for high-quality classroom observation processes that result in improved teaching and learning. However, one of the challenges with classroom observations is capacity. With the increasing numbers of part-time faculty, it becomes impossible for a few administrators or coordinators to regularly conduct classroom observations on all faculty members.

At many community colleges, the responsibility of evaluating all full and part-time faculty typically falls on the chairperson or faculty coordinator. This is only one of the many tasks the chairperson or coordinator must do and the sheer number of faculty in some departments makes this near impossible. Thus, it is not surprising to discover that many instructors are not being observed at all.

If they are being observed, these observations are not being conducted as frequently as desired. When classroom observations are being conducted, the pre-meeting and post-observation meetings may not be happening at all or only happening via e-mail communications because of time constraints. As a result, conversations about how to improve teaching and learning are not always being incorporated into the classroom observation process.

Addressing this capacity issue is of paramount importance. Colleges committed to student success need to prioritize teaching and learning and ensure this is the focus of campus leaders at all levels of academic affairs. Effective teaching is one of the best predictors of student achievement.

This may mean that job descriptions and duties might have to change in order for chairpersons or coordinators to have more time dedicated to conducting classroom observations. However, even if conducting classroom observations were the only responsibility of a chairperson or coordinator, there still might not be enough hours in the day to observe all faculty. Thus, they cannot do this task alone. Colleges will need to determine who else might support this process.

Faculty can conduct classroom observations. In fact, many colleges use a peer observation model. Most would agree that faculty are best positioned to provide suggestions and meaningful feedback to colleagues about teaching and learning. Full and part-time faculty who have a record of teaching excellence can be valuable members of the classroom observation team. There is much talent in the part-time faculty body that is often underutilized.

Colleges will want to invite both full and part-time faculty to trainings on how to conduct effective classroom observations. Because of the importance of this task and the time-consuming nature of it, colleges will want to determine how to motivate faculty to become observers. Despite faculty being interested in supporting colleagues and improving teaching, they have incredibly heavy teaching loads and other responsibilities. Colleges will likely need to decide what the best use of faculty time is outside of teaching and modify reward and compensation structures so that these priorities are communicated.

Some colleges look to Teaching and Learning Center staff to also conduct observations but capacity and role issues may pose a challenge. Teaching and Learning Centers do not typically have a large staff. In fact, most community colleges with a Teaching and Learning Center have less than one full-time person dedicated to this work (Beach, Sorcinelli, Austin, & Rivard, 2016). In most cases, a faculty member receives a reduced teaching load in exchange for their leadership of the Center. Thus, the Teaching and Learning Center director will not likely have much time for this activity given their other responsibilities.

Colleges may want to consider expanding the number of staff so that the Teaching and Learning Center can be more involved in conducting classroom observations. However, even if capacity is increased, it is important that Teaching and Learning Center tasks align with their purpose and mission of supporting faculty as they improve their teaching practices.

Classroom observations focused on improvement align nicely with these goals. Classroom observations that are conducted as a part of evaluation processes would not likely align with the Center's mission. Centers that provide this service to faculty typically only share observation reports with the instructor to ensure the observations do not become a part of evaluation portfolios unless the faculty member elects to include it.

REVIEW OF TEACHING MATERIALS

Another approach to assessing instructor effectiveness is a review of teaching materials. The syllabus is one of the most important teaching documents because it conveys the course learning outcomes and maps out the path for student learning. Assignments and PowerPoint slides are other examples of course materials that can be reviewed.

Syllabus

A syllabus review is an underutilized approach to instructor effectiveness. As discussed previously, the syllabus communicates the course design. It provides a window into the teaching and learning experience. Colleges can train a team of faculty and administrators on best practices related to syllabus design so that they can serve as syllabi reviewers. Review teams will likely want to use a rubric to evaluate the syllabus. This rubric can be shared widely with faculty.

A checklist-style rubric can be used to determine if all the essential information such as a course description, professor's contact hours, and materials was included. See Box 4.1 in chapter 4 for a sample syllabus checklist. However, colleges will also want to assess quality through an analytical rubric. For example, the rubric can address whether learning outcomes are measurable and explicitly linked to program goals and can also address whether the assignments have clearly explained rationales that connect back to learning outcomes. The tone, organization, and visual appeal of the syllabus can also be included in the rubric (Harrington & Thomas, 2018).

Assignments

Assignments are another teaching resource that can be reviewed. Reviewers can assess the clarity and rigor of the assignment. For example, reviewers can determine if the purpose and expectations of the assignment were clearly communicated to students. Reviewers can also assess whether the level of rigor aligns with the course level and learning outcomes.

Reviewers will also want to look for the connection between summative and formative assessments. Feedback on ways to improve the nature of the summative assignments so they more clearly align with the course learning outcomes and suggestions on how formative assessments can better connect to summative assessments can be shared with the instructor. Strategies to more clearly communicate expectations and faculty belief in students' ability to successfully complete assigned tasks can also be shared during this review process.

PowerPoint Slides

PowerPoint slides are a frequently used teaching tool. Reviewers can be trained in evidence-based multimedia practices so they can provide meaning-ful feedback to faculty on how to improve their PowerPoint slides. Based on extensive research, Mayer (2009) has shared several multimedia principles that should be used when developing and using PowerPoint slides. The most important finding is that slides that have one relevant image and just a few words describing the key point are most likely to lead to higher levels of learning.

PowerPoint slides can be reviewed to determine if the faculty member used research-based multimedia principles as a guide when developing the slides. The organizational structure of lessons can also be assessed to some extent by reviewing the slide sequence. Reviewers can assess whether the main points of the lesson are being communicated clearly and in a well-organized format.

Recommendations can be made to assist faculty with putting multimedia research into practice in their classroom. Faculty who have text-heavy slides can be encouraged to take this content and put it into a handout and create a more visually effective slide. Faculty may also find it helpful to create documents with the bulleted lists that were previously on the slides so that they can refer to this document as a resource when teaching. Colleges who include a review of PowerPoint slides as a strategy to assess instructor effectiveness can help faculty develop research-based visual aids.

FACULTY SELF-ASSESSMENT

Full-time faculty are often asked to conduct a self-evaluation, reflecting on their achievements and identifying areas for growth, as a part of reappoint-ment, tenure, and promotion processes. When engaging in the self-assess-ment process, faculty reflect on their accomplishments in teaching, service, and scholarship. Unfortunately, because this process is often connected to evaluation, faculty focus almost exclusively on examples of success. Reflection should involve not only assessing what worked but also what didn't work well.

Part-time faculty are often excluded or not required to participate in the self-reflective process. The current forms and templates being used may not be relevant to part-time faculty who do not typically have service and scholarship expectations. There may not be a formal reappointment process in place for part-time faculty either. As part-time faculty comprise a large portion of the overall teaching faculty, it is important that colleges modify forms and processes to assess and support part-time faculty.

Research has shown it is beneficial for faculty to engage in self-reflection about their teaching practices (Daniels, Pirayoff, & Bessant, 2013). The act of thinking about and responding to questions related to pedagogical and andragogical practices can result in faculty enhancing or modifying their teaching practices. Thus, colleges will want to ensure that self-assessment is incorporated into processes and practices related to assessing instructor effectiveness.

Colleges will need to determine how to best increase focus on reflection for improvement so that self-assessment reports contain successes and challenges. Using a more structured self-assessment approach that is centered on teaching and learning is advantageous. Colleges can provide faculty with a structured template that contains reflective questions on what worked well and what did not work well.

Colleges may also want to require full and part-time faculty to identify specific examples or evidence related to their responses. Faculty can be encouraged to engage in journaling throughout the year so that these examples are easy to identify. These strategies can be a powerful way for faculty to monitor their own growth and effectiveness with various teaching approaches.

The following are some sample questions that might be included in the teaching portion of the self-assessment process:

1. How do you help students know the value and relevance of learning tasks? How do you communicate the course learning outcomes to students?
2. How well do your assignments assess whether students have achieved the learning outcomes? Do final grades tell the story about whether a student has achieved the course learning outcomes? How do you know?
3. What teaching strategies do you use and how do you know if these are effective?

4. How do you determine whether a student is on track to successfully achieve the learning outcomes? What do you do to support students who are struggling?
5. What strategies do you use to engage your students? How do you know if they are engaged?
6. What modifications have you made to your teaching practices? Why?
7. How do your teaching practices and policies impact different student populations? How do you know this is the case?
8. What teaching challenges do you encounter? How do you address these challenges?
9. How can you grow as an educator? What areas of growth would you like to focus on this coming year? Why?
10. What are your "prouds"? What went really well? How do you know?

STUDENT ACHIEVEMENT DATA

Colleges will certainly want to track student performance data related to the achievement of course and program learning outcomes. In addition to collecting and reporting on student success outcomes of the general student body, colleges will also want to disaggregate data to determine the impact institutional teaching and learning efforts are having on populations that have historically underperformed. Faculty will want to see the impact of their efforts on student success rates.

It is important, however, for colleges and faculty to recognize there are many factors outside faculty members' control that impact learning. For example, a student may be in class with a faculty member who is consistently using evidence-based practices but because of a personal issue, the student may not be performing well academically. There are a wide range of factors that impact learning.

Faculty and colleges may become discouraged if the student success outcomes needle is not moving despite intentional, time-consuming efforts to improve teaching and learning. When attempting to understand the data, student success indicators should be interpreted with caution and with consideration for the many factors that impact student success. For these reasons, colleges should not rely exclusively on student data to assess instructor effectiveness.

CONCLUDING REMARKS

Assessing instructor effectiveness is important and can lead to improved teaching and learning when done well. There are a variety of assessment tools that can be used. Student evaluations are perhaps the most widely used tool, however, research shows that student evaluations are often not accurate if assessing the effectiveness of the instructor. Student evaluations can provide a window into the student experience which can be important and helpful, especially when used as one of several assessment tools.

The classroom observation is probably the most important and helpful tool that can be used to assess instructor effectiveness. Direct observational data combined with suggestions and meaningful conversations with colleagues will likely result in improved teaching and learning. A review of teaching materials can also provide faculty with helpful feedback that can be used to improve teaching and learning practices. Finally, asking faculty to engage in self-reflection is also important and can most certainly lead to improved teaching practices.

References

Almond, R. J. (2009). Group assessment: Comparing group and individual undergraduate module marks. *Assessment & Evaluation in Higher Education, 34*(2), 141–48. https://doi. org/10.1080/02602930801956083

Aloni, M., & Harrington, C. (2018). Research-based practices for improving the effectiveness of asynchronous online discussion boards. *Scholarship of Teaching and Learning in Psychology, 4*(4), 271–89.

American Association of University Professors. (2018, October 11). *Data snapshot: Contingent faculty in U.S. higher ed.* https://www.aaup.org/sites/default/files/10112018%20Data %20Snapshot%20Tenure.pdf

American Sociological Association. (2019, September). *Statement on student evaluations of teaching.* https://www.asanet.org/sites/default/files/asa_statement_on_student_evaluations_ of_teaching_sept52019.pdf

Anderson, L.. & Krathwohl, D. A. (2001). *Taxonomy for learning, teaching and assessing: A revision of Bloom's taxonomy of educational objectives.* Longman.

Armbruster, P., Patel, M., Johnson, E., & Weiss, M. (2009). Active learning and student centered pedagogy improve student attitudes and performance in introductory biology. *CBE—Life Sciences Education, 8*(3), 203–13.

Baeten, M., Dochy, F., & Struyven, K. (2013). The effects of different learning environments on student's motivation for learning and their achievement. *British Journal of Educational Psychology, 83*(3), 484–501.

Baker, S. (2012). Classroom karaoke. *Youth Studies Australia, 31*(1), 25–33.

Banachowski, G. (1997). *Advantages and disadvantages of employing part-time faculty in community colleges.* (ED405037). ERIC https://www.ericdigests.org/1997-4/part.htm

Banna, J., Grace Lin, M. F., Stewart, M., & Fialkowski, M. K. (2015). Interaction matters: Strategies to promote engaged learning in an online introductory nutrition course. *Journal of Online Learning and Teaching, 11*(2), 249–61. (ED405037). ERIC https://www.ericdigests. org/1997-4/part.htm

Beach, A. L., Sorcinelli, M. D., Austin, A. E., & Rivard, J. K. (2016). *Faculty development in the age of evidence.* Stylus Publishing.

Behar-Horenstein, L. S., Garvin, C. W., Catalanotto, F. A., & Hudson-Vassell, C. N. (2014). The role of needs assessment for faculty development. *Journal of Faculty Development, 28*(2), 75–86.

Benander, R. (2013). Redesigning course from the ground up: From outcomes to assessment to activities. In S. Sipple and R. Lightner (Eds.), *Developing faculty learning communities at two-year colleges: Collaborative models to improve teaching and learning* (pp. 60–76). Stylus Publishing.

Betts, S. C. (2008). Teaching and assessing basic concepts to advanced application: Using Bloom's taxonomy to inform graduate course design. *Academy of Educational Leadership Journal, 12*(3), 99–106.

Blessing, S. B., & Blessing, J. S. (2010). PsychBusters: A means of fostering critical thinking in the introductory course. *Teaching of Psychology, 37*(3), 178–82. https://doi.org/ 10.1080%2F00986283.2010.488540

Bloom, B. S. (Ed.). (1956). *Taxonomy of educational objectives: The classification of educational goals; Handbook I: Cognitive domain.* Longmans, Green, and Company.

Bombardieri, M. (2019, September 25). How to fix education's racial inequities, one tweak at a time. *Politico.* https://www.politico.com/agenda/story/2019/09/25/higher-educations-racial-inequities-000978

Brown, J., & Kurzweil, M. (2018). *Instructional quality, student outcomes, and institutional finances.* American Council on Education, Washington, DC. https://www.acenet.edu/ Documents/Instructional-Quality-Student-Outcomes-and-Institutional-Finances.pdf

Center for Community College Student Engagement. (2019). *A mind at work: Maximizing the relationship between mindset and student success (2019 national report).* https:// www.ccsse.org/NR2019/Mindset.pdf

Center for Community College Student Engagement. (2014). *Contingent commitments: Bringing part-time faculty into focus* (A special report from the Center for Community College Student Engagement). http://www.ccsse.org/docs/PTF_Special_Report.pdf

Clark, R. E., Kirschner, P. A., & Sweller, J. (2012). *Putting students on the path to learning: The case for fully guided instruction.* American Educator, 6–11. https://www.aft.org/sites/ default/files/periodicals/Clark.pdf

Community College Survey of Student Engagement (CCSSE). (2007). *Committing to student engagement: Reflections on CCSSE's first five years (2007 findings).* https://files.eric.ed. gov/fulltext/ED529080.pdf

Cox, M. (2004). Introduction to faculty learning communities. *New Directions for Teaching and Learning, 97*, 5–23. https://cms.ysu.edu/sites/default/files/documents/Introduction_to_ Faculty_Learning_Communities_by_Milt_Cox.pdf

Daniels, E., Pirayoff, R., & Bessant, S. (2013). Using peer observation and collaboration to improve teaching practices. *Universal Journal of Educational Research, 1*(3), 268–74.

Davis, M., & Hult, R. E. (1997). Effects of writing summaries as a generative learning activity during note taking. *Teaching of Psychology, 24*(1), 47.

Davys, D., & Jones, V. (2007). Peer observation: A tool for continuing professional development. *International Journal of Therapy & Rehabilitation, 14*(11), 489–93.

Dixon, J. S., Crooks, H., & Henry, K. (2006). Breaking the ice: Supporting collaboration and the development of community online. *Canadian Journal of Learning and Technology, 32*(2), 1–20.

Drew, S., & Klopper, C. (2014). Evaluating faculty pedagogic practices to inform strategic academic professional development: A case of cases. *Higher Education, 67*(3), 349–67.

Eggleston, T., & Smith, G. (2004). Building community in the classroom through ice-breakers and parting ways. *Society for the Teaching of Psychology, Office of Teaching Resources in Psychology.* http://teachpsych.org/resources/Documents/otrp/resources/eggleston04.pdf

Forgie, S. E., Yonge, O., & Luth, R. (2018). Centres for teaching and learning across Canada: What's going on? *Canadian Journal for the Scholarship of Teaching and Learning, 9*(1), 1–18.

Foster, D. A., & Hermann, A. D. (2011). Linking the first week of class to end-of-term satisfaction: Using a reciprocal interview activity to create an active and comfortable classroom. *College Teaching, 59*(3), 111–16.

Fuller, R. (2017). Conclusion: Toward making the invisible visible, heard, and valued. In R. Fuller, M. K. Brown, and K. Smith (Eds.). *Adjunct faculty voices: Cultivating professional development and community at the front lines of higher education.* Stylus Publishing.

Galbraith, C., & Merrill, G. (2012). Predicting student achievement in university-level business and economics classes: Peer observation of classroom instruction and student ratings of teaching effectiveness. *College Teaching, 60*(2), 48–55.

Gannon, K. (2016, August 3). *The absolute worst way to start the semester.* Chronical Vitae. https://chroniclevitae.com/news/1498-the-absolute-worst-way-to-start-the-semester

Gannon-Slater, N., Ikenberry, S., Jankowski, N., & Kuh, G. (2014, March). *Institutional assessment practices across accreditation regions.* National Institute for Learning Outcomes Assessment. https://www.learningoutcomeassessment.org/documents/Accreditation%20report.pdf

Garrison, D. R., Anderson, T., & Archer, W. (2000). Critical inquiry in a text-based environment: Computer conferencing in higher education. *The Internet and Higher Education, 2*(2–3), 87–105.

Gurung, R. A. R., Ansburg, P. I., Alexander, P. A., Lawrence, N. K., & Johnson, D. E. (2008). The state of the scholarship of teaching and learning in psychology. *Teaching of Psychology, 35*(4), 249–61.

Hanover Research. (2014, January). *Faculty mentoring models and effective practices.* Academy Administration Practice, 1–15. https://www.hanoverresearch.com/media/Faculty-Mentoring-Models-and-Effectives-Practices-Hanover-Research.pdf

Haras, C., Taylor, S. C., Sorcinelli, M. D., & von Hoene, L. (2017). *Institutional commitment to teaching excellence: Assessing the impacts and outcomes of faculty development.* American Council on Education.

Harnish, R. J., & Bridges, K. (2011). Effect of syllabus tone: Students' perceptions of instructor and course. *Social Psychology of Education: An International Journal, 14*(3), 319–30.

Harrington, C., & Thomas, M. (2018). *Designing a motivational syllabus: Creating a learning path for student engagement.* Stylus Publishing.

Harrington, C., & Zakrajsek, T. (2017). *Dynamic lecturing: Research-based strategies to enhance lecture effectiveness.* Stylus Publishing.

Hrepic, Z., Zollman, D., & Rebello, S. (2004). Students' understanding and perceptions of the content of a lecture. *AIP [American Institute of Physics Conference Proceedings, 720*(1), 189–92. https://doi.org/10.1063/1.1807286

Hutchings, P. (2010, April). *Opening doors to faculty involvement in assessment.* National Institute for Learning Outcomes Assessment, Occasional Paper, #4. https://learningoutcomesassessment.org/documents/PatHutchings_000.pdf

Jenkins, D., Lahr, H., Brown, A. E., & Mazzariello, A. (2019, September). *Redesigning your college through Guided Pathways: Lessons on managing whole-college reform from the AACC Pathways Project.* Community College Research Center, Teachers College, Columbia University. https://ccrc.tc.columbia.edu/media/k2/attachments/redesigning-your-college-guided-pathways.pdf

King, P. E., & Behnke, R. R. (2005). Problems associated with evaluating student performance in groups. *College Teaching, 53*(2), 57–61.

Kisker, C. B. (2019). *Enabling faculty-led student success efforts at community colleges.* American Council on Education, 1–17. https://www.acenet.edu/Documents/Enabling-Faculty-Led-Student-Success-Efforts.pdf

Knol, M. H., Veld, R. I., Vorst, H. C. M., van Driel, J. H., & Mellenbergh, G. J. (2013). Experimental effect of student evaluations coupled with collaborative consultation on college professors' instructional skills. *Research in Higher Education, 54*(8), 825–50.

Koc, E. W. (2011). Getting noticed, getting hired: Candidate attributes that recruiters seek. *NACE Journal, 72*(2), 14–19.

Komarraju, M., & Nadler, D. (2013). Self-efficacy and academic achievement: Why do implicit beliefs, goals, and effort regulation matter? *Learning and Individual Differences, 25,* 67–72.

Lang, J. M. (n.d.). *How to teach a good first day of class: Advice guide.* The Chronicle of Higher Education. https://www.chronicle.com/interactives/advice-firstday

League for Innovation in the Community College. (2018). *Untapped leaders: Faculty and the challenge of student completion.* https://www.league.org/sites/default/files/Untapped%20Leaders_Faculty%20and%20the%20Challenge%20of%20Student%20Completion_0.pdf

Lederman, D. (2018a, October 31). Conflicted views of technology: A survey of faculty attitudes. *Inside Higher Ed.* https://www.insidehighered.com/news/survey/conflicted-views-technology-survey-faculty-attitudes

Lederman, D. (2018b, November 7). Online education ascends. *Inside Higher Ed.* https://www.insidehighered.com/digital-learning/article/2018/11/07/new-data-online-enrollments-grow-and-share-overall-enrollment

Lenning, O. T., Hill, D. M., Saunders, K. P., Solan, A., & Stokes, A. (2013). *Powerful learning communities: A guide to developing student, faculty, and professional learning communities to improve student success and organizational effectiveness.* Stylus Publishing.

Lieberman, M. (2018, February 28). Centers of the pedagogical universe. *Inside Higher Ed.* https://www.insidehighered.com/digital-learning/article/2018/02/28/centers-teaching-and-learning-serve-hub-improving-teaching

Luo, L., Kiewra, K. A., & Samuelson, L. (2016). Revising lecture notes: How revision, pauses, and partners affect note taking and achievement. *Instructional Science: An International Journal of the Learning Sciences, 44*(1), 45–67. https://psycnet.apa.org/doi/10.1007/s11251-016-9370-4

Malu, K. F. (2015). Observation tools for professional development. *English Teaching Forum, 53*(1), 14–24. https://files.eric.ed.gov/fulltext/EJ1060238.pdf

Marsh, H. W. (2007). Do university teachers become more effective with experience? A multi-level growth model of students' evaluations of teaching over 13 years. *Journal of Educational Psychology, 99*(4), 775–90.

Mayer, R. E. (2009). *Multi-media learning, 2nd edition.* Cambridge University Press.

McClenney, K. M. (2007). Research update: The Community College Survey of Student Engagement. *Community College Review, 35*(2), 137–46. https://doi.org/10.1177%2F0091552107306583

McConnell, K. D., & Rhodes, T. L. (2017). *On solid ground: VALUE report 2017.* Association of American Colleges and Universities. https://www.aacu.org/value

McCullough, C. A., & Jones, E. (2014). Creating a culture of faculty participation in assessment: Factors that promote and impede satisfaction. *Journal of Assessment and Institutional Effectiveness, 4*(1), 85–101.

McGinley, J. J., & Jones, B. D. (2014). A brief instructional intervention to increase students' motivation on the first day of class. *Teaching of Psychology, 41*(2), 158–62.

Mellow, G. O., & Heelan, C. M. (2014). Financing community college. In *Minding the dream: The process and practice of the American community college, 2nd edition* (pp. 27–56). Rowman & Littlefield.

Millis, B. J. (2002). *Enhancing learning—and more! Through cooperative learning.* IDEA Paper #38, 1–10. http://www.theideacenter.org/sites/default/files/IDEA_Paper_38.pdf

Morris, L. V., Xu, H., & Finnegan, C. L. (2005). Roles of faculty in teaching asynchronous undergraduate courses. *Journal of Asynchronous Learning Networks, 9*(1), 65–82.

Nicol, D. J., & Macfarlane-Dick, D. (2006). Formative assessment and self-regulated learning: A model and seven principles of good feedback practice. *Studies in Higher Education, 31*(2), 199–218.

Palmer, M. S. (2017, June). *The science of transparency* [Conference session]. Lilly Teaching and Learning Conference, Bethesda, MD. https://www.lillyconferences-md.com/

Pando, P. (2019, July 28). *Taking action to promote equity* [Conference session]. The Community College Showcase: Promoting Equity and Student Success, Jersey City, New Jersey.

Payette, P. R., & Brown, M. K. (2018). *Gathering mid-semester feedback: Three variations to improve instruction.* IDEA Paper #76, 1–7. https://www.ideaedu.org/Portals/0/Uploads/Documents/IDEA%20Papers/IDEA%20Papers/PaperIDEA_67.pdf

Penn, J. (2007, June 26). Assessment for "us" and assessment for "them." *Inside Higher Ed.* http://www.insidehighered.com/views/2007/06/26/assessment-us-and-assessment-them

Perez, A. M., McShannon, J., & Hynes, P. (2012). Community college faculty development program and student achievement. *Community College Journal of Research and Practice, 36*(5), 379–85. https://doi.org/10.1080/10668920902813469

Perrine, R. M., Lisle, J., & Tucker, D. L. (1995). Effects of a syllabus offer of help, student age, and class size on college students' willingness to seek support from faculty. *Journal of Experimental Education, 64*(1), 41–52.

Prichard, J. S., Stratford, R. J., & Bizo, L. A. (2006). Team-skills training enhances collaborative learning. *Learning and Instruction, 16*(3), 256–65. https://doi.org/10.1016/j.learninstruc.2006.03.005

Ran, F., & Bickerstaff, S. (2019, September 30). *Supporting the supporters: Empowering adjuncts to promote student success.* Community College Research Center, Teachers College, Columbia University. https://ccrc.tc.columbia.edu/easyblog/empowering-adjuncts-student-success.html

Ran, F. X., & Xu, D. (2017). *How and why do adjunct instructors affect students' academic outcomes? Evidence from two-year and four-year colleges* (CAPSEE working paper). Center for Analysis of Postsecondary Education and Employment.

Reynolds, H. L., & Kearns, K. D. (2017). A planning tool for incorporating backward design, active learning, and authentic assessment in the college classroom. *College Teaching, 65*(1), 17–27.

Rhoades, G. (2012). *Faculty engagement to enhance student attainment.* Paper prepared for National Commission on Higher Education Attainment. https://www.acenet.edu/Documents/Faculty-Engagement-to-Enhance-Student-Attainment--Rhoades.pdf

Rhodes, T. L. (2010). *Assessing outcomes and improving achievement: Tips and tools for using rubrics.* Association of American Colleges and Universities.

Robinson, D. (2019). Engaging students on the first day of class: Student-generated questions promote positive course expectations. *Scholarship of Teaching and Learning in Psychology, 5*(3), 183–88.

Robles, M. M. (2012). Executive perceptions of the top 10 soft skills needed in today's workplace. *Business Communication Quarterly, 75*(4), 453–65.

Ruhl, K., Hughes, C., & Schloss, P. (1987). Using the pause procedure to enhance lecture recall. *Teacher Education and Special Education, 10*(1), 14–18.

Sarfo, F., & Ellen, J. (2011). Investigating the impact of positive resource interdependence and individual accountability on students' academic performance in cooperative learning. *Electronic Journal of Research in Educational Psychology, 9*(1), 73–93.

Schroeder, C. M. (2011). *Coming in from the margins.* Stylus Publishing.

Shugart, S. (2018, September 26). *Student success factors* [Conference session]. The Two Year First Year Conference, Orlando, FL. https://tyfy.info/

Smith, A. (2007). Professional development issues for community colleges. *Peer Review, 9*(4). Association of American Colleges and Universities. https://www.aacu.org/publications-research/periodicals/professional-development-issues-community-colleges

Stark, P. B., & Freishtat, R. (2014, September). An evaluation of course evaluations. *ScienceOpen, 1,* 1–26. http:/doi:10.14293/S2199-1006.1.SOR-EDU.AOFRQA.v1

Stout, K. A. (2018, November 28). *The urgent case: Focusing the next generation of community college redesign on teaching and learning.* The 2018 Dallas Herring Lecture, North Carolina State University. https://www.achievingthedream.org/resource/17642/the-urgent-case-focusing-the-next-generation-of-community-college-redesign-on-teaching-and-learning

Suskie, L. (2018). *Assessing student learning: A common sense guide, 2nd edition.* John Wiley & Sons.

Swan, K., Matthews, D., Bogle, L., Boles, E., & Day, S. (2012). Linking online course design and implementation to learning outcomes: A design experiment. *Internet and Higher Education,* 81–88. http:/doi:10.1016/j.iheduc.2011.07.002

Thompson, J. (2006). Best practices in asynchronous online course discussions. *Journal of College Teaching and Learning, 3*(7), 19–30.

Thurston, L. P., Navarrete, L., & Miller, T. (2009). A ten-year faculty mentoring program: Administrator, mentor, and mentee perspectives. *The International Journal of Learning, 16,* 1–18.

References

Van den Bergh, L., Ros, A., & Beijaard, D. (2014). Improving teacher feedback during active learning: Effects of a professional development program. *American Educational Research Journal, 51*(4), 772–809.

Vander Schee, B. A. (2007). Setting the stage for active learning: An interactive marketing class activity. *Marketing Education Review, 17*(1), 63–67.

Walker, I., & Crogan, M. (1998). Academic performance, prejudice, and the jigsaw classroom: New pieces to the puzzle. *Journal of Community & Applied Social Psychology, 8*(6), 381–93.

Wiggins, G., & McTighe, J. (2005). *Understanding by design, expanded 2nd edition*. Pearson.

Wininger, S. R. (2005). Using your tests to teach: Formative summative assessment. *Teaching of Psychology, 32*(3), 164–66. http:/doi:10.1207/s15328023top3203_7

Wyner, J. (2019, June 12). *The president's role in improving teaching and learning*. Community College Research Center, Teachers College, Columbia University. https://ccrc.tc.columbia.edu/easyblog/presidents-role-improving-teaching-learning.html

Yu, H., Campbell, D., & Mendoza, P. (2015). The relationship between the employment of part time faculty and student degree and/or certificate completion in two-year community colleges. *Community College Journal of Research and Practice, 39*(11), 986–1006. http:/doi:10.1080/10668926.2014.918910

Zakrajsek, T. (2016). Oh, the places your center can go: Possible programs to offer. *Journal on Centers for Teaching and Learning, 8*, 93–109.

About the Author

Christine Harrington is an associate professor and co-coordinator for a new EdD in Community College Leadership Program at New Jersey City University, a program that focuses on developing leaders at all levels. Prior to joining NJCU, Dr. Harrington served a two-year term as the executive director of the Center for Student Success at the New Jersey Council of County Colleges where she assisted all nineteen community colleges in New Jersey with implementing Guided Pathways and improving student success outcomes. In this position, she championed faculty engagement in Guided Pathways at the state and national level. Most of Dr. Harrington's career has been as a practitioner leader in the community college sector. She worked at Middlesex County College in Edison, New Jersey, for more than eighteen years in several different roles, including professor of psychology, director of the Center for the Enrichment of Learning and Teaching, coordinator of the Student Success course, assessment coordinator, counselor, and disability services provider. Dr. Harrington also provides coaching and consulting services to community colleges engaged in Guided Pathways. She earned her BA in psychology and MA in counseling and personnel services from The College of New Jersey and her PhD in counseling psychology from Lehigh University.

She is a national expert on student success, the first-year seminar, teaching and learning, and Guided Pathways. Dr. Harrington is the author of *Student Success in College: Doing What Works!* 3rd edition, a research-based first-year seminar textbook that is aligned with Guided Pathways. She also co-authored the following books: *Why the First-Year Seminar Matters: Helping Students Choose and Stay on a Career Path* (with Theresa Orosz), *Dynamic Lecturing: Research-Based Strategies to Enhance Lecture Effectiveness* (with Todd Zakrajsek), and *Designing a Motivational Syllabus:*

Creating a Learning Path for Student Engagement (with Melissa Thomas). She frequently keynotes and presents at local, regional, and national conferences and has been an invited speaker at more than fifty colleges and universities. She shares numerous teaching and learning resources on her website: www.scholarlyteaching.org.